In memory of the
Greatest Generation.
Herschel Hill

HICK FROM THE STICKS

Texas Farm Life in the Thirties

HERSCHEL HILL

D1453796

"Hick From The Sticks: Texas Farm Life in the Thirties," by Herschel Hill. ISBN 978-1-60264-566-0 (softcover); 978-1-60264-567-7 (ebook).

Published 2010 by Virtualbookworm.com Publishing Inc., P.O. Box 9949, College Station, TX 77842, US. ©2010, Herschel Hill. All rights reserved. No part of this publication may be reproduced, stored in a retrieval system, or transmitted in any form or by any means, electronic, mechanical, recording or otherwise, without the prior written permission of Herschel Hill.

Manufactured in the United States of America.

CONTENTS

Also by Herschel Hill

Looking Toward Eternity: A Life Hereafter?

America, A House Divided

Pleasing God: The Jesus Agenda

Fighting Over Faith

A Word from the Author

This book is my story, my life on a farm in the piney woods country of Northeast Texas during the thirties and forties. But, it is also the life of millions of other farm kids across the South during that time period. We called a multitude of places home, our extended families were different, we raised a variety of crops, each had unique life experiences, and our cultures were tied to the geographical regions wherein we lived. Nonetheless, the things we had in common far outweighed our differences.

I grew up during the aftermath of the Great Depression, so I saw firsthand and lived the hardships of that time period. The Great Depression commenced in 1929, three years before my birth, and hung on some ten years. Parents of my generation eked out a meager living by the sweat of their brow on small family farms. Cotton was king in those days, although farmers in some regions of the South raised other crops. Farmers did all the work manually with the aid of horse-drawn farm implements.

Parents labored from dawn until dusk trying to feed and clothe their families. Offspring toiled beside parents to help produce sufficient family income to keep a roof over their heads, clothes on their backs, and food on the table. Children's education was not a high priority for a lot of farm folks during the twenties, thirties, and forties. People struggled to keep their heads above water financially, so parents often kept kids out of school to help with farm work. Farming was all most folks knew back then, so many farmers failed to appreciate the value of, and need for, an education for their children.

My generation grew up without automated power-driven farm equipment, electricity, running water, indoor bathrooms, air conditioning, telephones, television, computers, fancy houses, nice clothes, and oftentimes automobiles. Yet we survived and led happy, contented, and peaceful lives. We accepted hard work as a way of life, learned contentment with few worldly possessions, made do with what little we had, and did not envy neighbors perhaps better off than we were. All were poor but did not realize it.

To what, or to whom, can we attribute such a satisfying and fulfilling existence in the midst of hardship and trials? All credit belongs to our parents and their generation. They sacrificed for our well-being, taught us the value of hard work, instilled in us valuable character traits which benefit us throughout our lives, and struggled to provide a better life for us than the one they enjoyed. Folks today refer to our parents as the Greatest Generation, or the noble generation, and they richly deserve that title.

The cultures, events, family lore, struggles, recollections, and people described in the pages of this book represent my experiences growing up on a farm. Personal stories, anecdotes, and experiences bring the customs and way of life in that period of our nation's history down to a personal level. As I penned these words, my searching mind uncovered and revealed events, customs, and people long forgotten. Please join me as I relive my adolescent and teen years in rural East Texas, because it could very well be your life or that of your parents or grandparents.

I would like to express my appreciation to an aunt and cousins who shared their fond memories and anecdotes from our lives together some seventy years ago. Thank you, Aunt Juanita, Vaudine, Christine, Mildred, Hubert, Helen, Doyle, Harold, Kenneth, and Edgar for your contributions to my journey into the past. You are a cherished part of that past, as well as a welcome part of the present.

1.

The Culture

V eterans of World War II, the war that would end all wars, are a vanishing breed. Their numbers are dwindling as that generation dies off at a rapid rate. No generation since theirs has endured the hardships they faced during the Great Depression, suffered such horrific loss of life fighting a long bloody war on foreign soil, sacrificed to ensure their children and grandchildren would enjoy better lives than they experienced, and gave generously to rebuild the very nations they had fought so hard to conquer. Some folks call theirs the noble generation. Our predecessors exhibited the character, patriotism, courage, selflessness, tenacity, resourcefulness, and compassion we can only dream about. How was such a generation of heroes produced? Let us search for that answer in the pages of this book.

America in the twenties and thirties was a mix of urban dwellers and rural inhabitants, but the percentage of our population living on farms then was much higher than it is today. This book focuses generally on rural life in the South during the twenties and thirties, but specifically on farm life in the piney woods country of Northeast Texas during that time period. This author is a product of that culture, and most of the accounts contained in these pages are based on first-hand knowledge. Names are sometimes changed herein to hide the identities of individuals mentioned and shield them from possible embarrassment. A lot of the customs and actions which were normal and expected for that time period would be ridiculed and frowned on today.

I was born in 1932 and raised in the rural Cass County community of Knight's Bluff, adjacent to Antioch (Anti) community to the South, Blalock community to the Southeast, and the vast Sulphur River bottom land to the West and North. The nearest towns were Queen City and Atlanta, both roughly ten miles away. The entire region congregated to those two small towns to shop and do business. Prior to the war, farming was the primary occupation for the entire Ark-La-Tex region. A few people worked in logging and sawmills; others were employed in businesses in Texarkana, Atlanta, and Queen City; still others taught school; some held refinery and rough-necking jobs in the oil fields of Louisiana; a lot of men worked on WPA (Work Projects Administration) and CCC (Civilian Conservation Corps) projects funded by the federal government; and a few earned their living making and selling moonshine whiskey. But virtually everyone in my neck of the woods either lived on a farm or had lived on one at some time in the past.

Cass County was cotton and corn country back then; cotton was the money crop, and corn was the feed crop. Everyone raised milk cows and chickens, so milk, butter, and eggs were plentiful, and a majority of the people feasted on chicken for Sunday dinner. Every household raised hogs, which were butchered at the first cold spell to provide meat for the year. Each farm contained a large vegetable patch and a fruit orchard as well. The vegetables, fruit, and an abundant supply of wild berries were canned, preserved, or dried for year-round consumption. Squirrel hunting and fishing were popular sports for a lot of folks, and that fish and game constituted another source of meat for many families. Money was in very short supply during and after the Great Depression, so people in the thirties ate what they raised for the most part. Store-bought groceries were kept to an absolute minimum.

Farming in the thirties was vastly different from the high-tech agriculture of today. Family farms typically consisted of fifty to one hundred acres each, depending on how many children were available to share in the work. Large families owned large farms. A majority of the people owned their farms, but tenant farms like the one I grew up on were also plentiful. The owner of a tenant farm split the cost of seeds, fertilize, and insecticides with the farmer. The farmer performed the work, and the two shared in the harvest. The owner received one-third of the corn crop and one-fourth of the proceeds from sale of the cotton harvest. All farm work was performed manually, utilizing horses and mules rather than tractors and other motor-driven equipment.

The roads were unpaved in the area where we lived. Most were narrow dirt roads with deep ditches on each side, so driving on slick muddy roads in rainy weather was difficult and oftentimes dangerous. A common occurrence was older boys piling out of a school bus to help push the bus up a slick muddy hill after a rain. Getting your shoes muddy, if you wore shoes at all, was not a major concern when I was growing up. Can you imagine kids today helping to push an under-powered Ford Model T car up a steep hill with the mother driving? I have been there and done that. Meeting or passing another car on those narrow dirt roads was quite a challenge, especially after a heavy downpour.

Our houses were simple wood frame structures with either galvanized tin or wood shingle roofs. An open hallway sometimes separated the bedrooms from the rest of the house, and most houses had front and back porches. The house exteriors utilized rough unpainted lumber with wide 12-inch vertical boards and narrow 4-inch boards to cover the cracks, although a significant number of houses incorporated horizontal exterior boards. Most houses did not incorporate insulation, and quite often the houses did not include interior walls. You can imagine how cold an unheated bedroom was in the dead of winter. It was not uncommon to lie in bed and see daylight through the wall cracks and feel a cold draft through the openings. When nature called on cold nights, you either ventured out into the freezing porch or yard or used the "slop jars" (metal buckets) found in all homes. The women used the slop jars and the men braved the cold front or back porch.

Most communities, including ours, did not have electrical service in the thirties; that was prior to Rural Electric Administration (REA) power lines. Houses were lighted with kerosene (coal oil) lamps; we drew water from deep wells by bucket; houses were heated by wood-burning fireplaces or heaters; we cooked our meals on wood-burning stoves; our air conditioning was open windows; the women and girls used the potty in outhouses; the men and boys relieved themselves behind the barn; and Sears & Roebuck catalogues were put to good use in the outhouses.

If you are wondering about the men behind the barn, they found an ample supply of corn cobs to be quite useful. We used the red cobs for the dirty work and the white ones to verify a job well done. Discussions about sexual matters were off-limits in my household, so being a boy and an only child I possessed very little knowledge about girl things. I was dumb! I learned later in life, however, that girls did not have access to sanitary napkins back then. They utilized washable and reusable rags during their monthly periods. People utilized the resources available to them when I was growing up.

Education was not a high priority for most folks in the early 1900s. Very few of my parents' peers graduated from high school, a majority did not complete elementary school, and quite a few did not go to school at all. My father and mother completed the eighth and fifth grades, respectively. My generation was the first to graduate from high school in significant numbers. Many of my classmates dropped out of school early each spring to help plant the crops and then started school late in the summer in order to help with the harvesting. I was one of the lucky ones. My parents seldom pulled me out of school to help with the farming, so I was able to graduate from high school in 1947. I obtained an electrical engineering degree several years later, thanks to my Air Force service and the G.I. Bill.

Small rural schools were the norm during that time period, rather than large consolidated schools. Tiny one-room one-teacher or two-room two-teacher elementary schools served communities located three to four miles apart. All students walked to those elementary schools, some having to hoof it up to two miles, but we never skipped school because of inclement weather. School buses transported high school students to either Queen City or Atlanta, a distance of up to ten miles. Most school bus drivers picked up students on two separate routes each morning and afternoon, so a lot of the students left home before daylight in the morning and did not get home until nearly dark in the evening. And, none of the school buses were air conditioned in those days.

A significant number of rural folks did not own automobiles prior to World War II. They usually walked or relied on family and friends to take them places, but they sometimes rode in horse-drawn wagons or on horseback. Privately-owned school buses also picked up people on the school routes and took them to Queen City and Atlanta for all-day shopping on Saturday each week. The woman of the house, and perhaps one or more of the children, rode the school bus to town and bought staple groceries, household goods, clothing, and feed for livestock and chickens. An ice cream cone and candy bar, or perhaps a cowboy movie at the picture show in Atlanta, were special treats for the kids. I fondly remember those Saturday cowboy movies starring Roy Rogers, Gene Autry, The Durango Kid, the Three Musketeers, Lash Larue, and others.

I grew up in an all-white Southern community with no Hispanic, Jewish, or Catholic residents, so prejudice and discrimination were inherent in our culture. We were openly prejudiced against anyone "different" from us, including African Americans, Hispanics, Native Americans, Gypsies, Jews, and Catholics. A significant number of African Americans resided in adjacent communities, so prejudice against black people was most pronounced. White folks abused them verbally and physically, but most importantly, we made them feel like second class citizens with no dignity or self-worth.

Black delivery truck drivers refused to deliver construction material and farm products to the Knight's Bluff community, and African American farm workers refused to hire out to Knight's Bluff farmers. They were afraid to set foot in the community. Knight's Bluff community was referred to as "Blue Bucket Country," but I never learned the origin of that name. I was told that some white men shot at a group of black people one day while they were fishing on Sulphur River. That prejudice against people who were different is one aspect of my upbringing for which I am ashamed, and I trust and pray that I have overcome that prejudice in my adult years.

My family and neighbors were Protestant, and most of them practiced either Baptist, Methodist, Pentecost, or Mormon faith. Folks back then were God-fearing and religious, but they spent little time practicing their religion in community with other Christians. Pastors of rural churches were bi-vocational, and they normally pastored two churches. They preached at one church on the first and third Sundays of each month and preached at a different church on the second and fourth Sundays; they spent the fifth Sunday with families. That was the norm for Antioch Baptist Church where my family worshiped. Week-long revivals were popular, and the entire community turned out for whatever revival was being held at the time. It did not matter if it was your faith or not.

Rural families in the twenties and thirties were large, typically with four or more children. My father was one of eight siblings, and my mother had eight brothers and sisters, quite normal for families in those days. A one-kid family like mine was atypical for that time period. Farm boys looked forward to owning their own farm someday and starting a family, and they oftentimes settled on or near their family farms after marriage. Career choices for farm girls were limited. A young girl either stayed at home and worked on her father's farm or married, worked on her husband's farm, and had babies. That was some career choice, right ladies? Most farm girls chose to marry at a young age, typically in their teens. My mother married at age sixteen, for example, but a large percentage of girls from the farm married before age sixteen.

Farm life was hard, money was scarce, and we were somewhat isolated in rural communities with minimal transportation. You are probably thinking, "What a boring life, how could you have any fun as a kid?" Believe it or not, we were happy, and we did enjoy life. Our social life revolved around our extended families, and to some extent our churches. We worked long hard hours, but families shared meals together, and we spent most evenings playing games with our parents, brothers and sisters, cousins, or neighbors. We did not have televisions, telephones, or video games, but we did have battery-powered console radios to listen to and good books to read. Those were relaxing and beneficial activities.

Most young people did not own cars, they had no money to spend, they were dispersed around the community, and they lived up to ten miles from the nearest town, so what kind of social life did the young people of the thirties have? Were they able to date, and where did they go on dates? Four of my older cousins, Vaudine, Christine, Mildred, and Hubert, enlightened me on those questions. Young people usually dated in groups, and they walked or rode in a wagon unless one of the boys owned a car. Quite often, the group just walked down the road and talked; couples did not have a lot of privacy back then. Young people also attended church revivals, pie suppers, church socials, and parties and dances at people's homes. A lot of parents did not allow their daughters to go to dances, however, because of the alcohol consumed there.

Remember also that the guys walked up to three miles to "pick up" their dates and then walked home after dropping them off. Dating was not easy for country kids without wheels. A fire lookout tower near the Antioch Baptist Church was a popular hangout for young people in the thirties and forties. It was located on top of the highest hill in the vicinity so the forest ranger could spot smoke from fires anywhere in the region. The climb to the small room atop the tower was invigorating, and the view from the tower was exhilarating. I climbed that tower a few times when I was a young teenager.

Fire Lookout Tower

Folks spent Sundays in church, visiting back and forth with aunts and uncles, and/or visiting grandparents. It was such a joy to share a meal and fellowship with our extended family after a hard week of work. Cousins developed a closeness not seen in today's hectic and high-tech society. Our lifestyles were very similar, we shared common interests, and we were not burdened down with all the cares and concerns of today's society. We had arguments, spats, and even fights at times, but our love for one another and joy of being together never diminished. Church socials included pie suppers, covered-dish church dinners, Sunday School parties, and similar activities, and all age groups attended most socials. We worked together, played together, and worshiped together as families.

I am thankful and proud of the legacy left by my parents' generation, as well as the character traits instilled in me in my youth. Some folks from humble beginnings like mine seem to be apologetic and ashamed of the culture and environment in which they were reared. But I am convinced that enduring those difficult times, working hard like we did, facing the hardships we experienced, learning to live and be happy with less, treating everyone with honesty and integrity, and receiving guidance and encouragement from loving parents made a tremendous difference in my life. I count my humble background as a positive rather than a negative, and in no way do I want to deny or discredit the heritage left to me by my parents and grandparents. My desire and prayer is that I can leave a similar legacy for my daughter and grandchildren.

The remainder of this book examines various aspects of farm life in the twenties, thirties, and forties. It focuses on my personal experiences growing up, but also includes descriptions of farm life, churches, schools, the economy, families, racial prejudices, and recreational activities of that era. Anecdotes bring the customs of that time period down to a personal level. Forgive me if some of the descriptions and events drawn from my memory of that long-ago time period are not entirely accurate. I relate them to you as I remember them, and hopefully you will obtain a clear vision of what farm life was all about during the Great Depression and World War II.

2.

Family Life

R ural families in the twenties and thirties were large relative to today's average family size. Extended families tended to live in close proximity, and family settings were central to social life. Grayden Hill and Esther Brown Hill, both natives of Cass County, Texas, were my parents. Daddy was one of eight siblings, six of which survived to adulthood. All six resided and expired within a ten-mile radius of their birthplace. All of their offspring grew up together, worshiped in the same churches, spent most Sundays visiting with kinfolk, and played together. Virtually everything we did was somehow connected with our immediate family or our extended family.

My Parents

Four of my Hill clan cousins were my approximate age, three boys and one girl, and we developed a close relationship during our adolescent years. Our parents visited Grandma Hill most Sundays, so Doyle, Bonnie, Edgar, Harold, and I spent many joyful days together in our early years. Bonnie visited with girlfriends quite often on Sundays, so the four of us boys engaged in rough and tumble male activities most of the time. We did not have television, video games, bicycles, boom boxes, or any of the high-tech gadgets cherished by the youth of today, but we found plenty of fun things to do. Those activities are discussed in subsequent pages of this book.

Mother had eight brothers and sisters, and they too raised families within ten miles of their birthplace. I fondly remember visiting back and forth with aunts, uncles, and cousins, as well as attending occasional family get-togethers on Sundays. The Brown extended family was huge. Mama Brown claimed ninety-two grandchildren, great-grandchildren, and great-great-grandchildren when she died at age ninety-two. I was the third oldest of those ninety-two grandchildren, so I spent more time with Helen, Kenneth, and Wayne than I did with my younger cousins. The four of us attended Knight's Bluff School and visited back and forth with one another regularly, so we developed a close bond. I did spend a significant amount of time with a few of my other cousins as well, including Howard, Carroll, Marie, and Jean, but seldom got to see the younger ones because I moved to Louisiana shortly after graduation from high school.

A family get-together with a meal during my childhood was a lot different than it is today. The cooking was accomplished by the hostess in a hot kitchen on a wood-burning cook stove with open windows for air conditioning. The kitchen/dining area of a typical large-family house featured an unpainted wooden table with benches along the sides to accommodate twelve to fifteen people at one sitting. The men and older ladies ate first at large family meals, the other ladies ate next, and the kids ate last. Can you imagine telling kids today to wait for the adults to be served before they eat? I well remember standing around with cousins watching the adults eat and hoping a few good pieces of chicken would be left for us. The choice pieces were usually gone before our turn at the table.

Also ladies, how would you like to kill, pluck, and clean chickens for thirty to forty dinner guests, gather and prepare fresh vegetables for such a crowd, bake homemade biscuits and cornbread to feed them, and bake homemade pies and cakes for dessert? And then, to top it off, the ladies washed all the pots, pans, silverware, and dishes by hand using water heated on the cook stove. Mama Brown, with her huge extended family, faced that daunting task almost every Sunday, and the weekdays were not much better with her raising nine children. The men worked hard during the week, but they had it made on Sunday. They sat around and talked while the ladies prepared the meal and cleaned up afterward.

I remember one time when several of us planned to spend the night with Mama Brown and Daddy Brown, including an uncle and three cousins. Uncle Ray D began teasing and picking on Kenneth and me, par for the course for some of my uncles. Kenneth and I got tired of the teasing and decided to walk to his house and spend the night. It was late and very dark, but we took a shortcut through the woods, about a one-mile trek. We elected to bypass the dirt road because it passed by a house with mean dogs. I had no idea where the minimal trail ran, but Kenneth led the way with me holding tightly to his shoulder; I could not see him even though he was scarcely two feet in front of me. It was pitch dark in those woods, especially in a creek bottom we passed through, and boy was I scared. Kenneth did not seem to be afraid, so I put on a brave front. We finally made it to his house, to my relief, and we enjoyed a good night of sleep.

Families in the twenties and thirties took care of their own. A widowed grandmother often lived with one of her children. Grandma Hill resided with my parents the first few years of their marriage, and believe it or not, she slept in the same bedroom with them. Most houses back then contained large bedrooms which accommodated two or more beds, and the entire family sometimes occupied the same bedroom. And in a lot of homes, the living room doubled as a bedroom. I have often wondered how I came into this world with my grandmother sleeping in the same room with my parents.

A widowed grandmother oftentimes resided in her own home if it was near one of her children. One of her grandchildren could then stay with her at night so she would not be alone. If her own home was a significant distance from any of her offspring, however, they often built her a small house adjacent to one of theirs so they could look after her. That is precisely what happened with Grandma Hill. Daddy and one of his brothers, Uncle Charlie, who lived near us, constructed a small house for her close to theirs. My cousins and I then took turns staying with her at night, and her sons checked on her each day. I remember well the day Grandma Hill passed away in her own home with her children gathered around.

Mama Brown lived in her own home after both Daddy Brown and her second husband, Mr. Hillis, passed away. Her house was a relatively short distance from two of her sons' homes, but a number of her grandchildren took turns living with her. One or the other of them stayed with her fulltime for several years, except for time in school. Later as her health failed, three of her daughters took turns staying with her after she was unable to care for herself. Mother took Mama Brown into her home the final months of her life and cared for her with the help of her second husband, Homer, and Aunt Pauline. Folks took care of their parents and grandparents in those days; that was an obligation they did not shirk.

Newly wed couples faced a dilemma in the thirties and early forties. Most of them did not own automobiles, they had very little money, and the few motels were widely scattered, so they were unable to drive to a nearby city or motel for a "honeymoon." A lot of couples turned to extended family members for lodging that first night. I remember uncles spending their wedding nights with us. Our house was divided by a hallway, and my parents and I slept in a bedroom near the kitchen. Our spare bedroom across the hallway provided privacy, and it was available for guests, so it was ideal for newly wed couples.

One of my older cousins, Christine, tells me Clyde and she spent their wedding night with us in 1938, but I do not recall that incident. They borrowed Grandma Hill's car to find a minister to marry them, and they sat in the car with friends while the minister performed the wedding. They drove back to our house to spend their first night together. After paying the minister, Clyde had seventeen dollars and fifty cents. Their start to married life may seem strange today, and their financial condition sounds extreme, but that was the norm in the thirties.

People in the thirties also helped kinfolk and neighbors in times of crisis. If a farmer was unable to keep up with his farm work due to an illness or injury, his extended family lent a helping hand. That assistance was for only a few days at times, but at other times it was for an extended time period. Folks did not have home insurance prior to World War II, so loss of a dwelling place or barn to fire or a tornado was a major catastrophe. If a family lost their home due to such a disaster, their extended family and neighbors chipped in to help them rebuild. One of my uncle's home was annihilated by a deadly tornado, but the Red Cross, family, and friends helped him replace it. Generosity and compassion were simply part of the culture in my youth.

Most rural families were quite large, but they often employed resident hired hands to assist with the farm work. A resident hired hand resided with the family and received free room and board plus a small stipend. Hired help on the farm was usually a relative, for example a cousin or nephew. Young men hired out at times because of financial difficulties within their immediate families, but they hired out at other times to earn a little money of their own. Folks occasionally took in and raised children belonging to a relative because that family simply did not have the means to raise the children themselves. I do not know the particular circumstances, but Daddy employed one of his nephews to help during the farming season for one or two years. I am confident the arrangement was mutually beneficial, and I enjoyed those months spent with Charles.

Farm families worked together at times in performing large tasks. I remember Uncle Charlie and his son Doyle working with Daddy and me harvesting corn and watermelons, cutting firewood and stove wood for the winter, cleaning water wells, doing construction projects, butchering hogs, and working on various other tasks. Daddy and I helped them with their farm work, and Uncle Charlie and Doyle reciprocated by helping us with ours. Both men and women joined together at times in significant undertakings. One such job was gathering and canning vegetables, fruits, and berries, an ongoing activity during the growing season.

We enjoyed an abundant supply of vegetables, fruits, and wild berries in season, but we had to make provision for the off-season when fresh produce was not available. We could not run down to the grocery store and buy fresh produce. That meant we had to can, preserve, or dry produce for year-round use. Each family prepared several hundred jars of vegetables, fruits, pickles, jellies, and preserves, not a small task. The men and boys gathered corn, peas, tomatoes, green beans, cucumbers, okra, turnip greens, and other vegetables. The men and all the kids pitched in to clean, shell, snap, peel, shuck, and otherwise prepare the vegetables for canning. The ladies then labored in a hot kitchen canning the vegetables in a pressure cooker on a wood-burning cook stove. My older cousin, Vaudine, who lived near us, sometimes worked with Mother in the hot kitchen canning vegetables in two pressure cookers. Much of the fruit was canned in the same manner, whereas other fruits and berries were made into preserves and jellies.

Dried fruit was also a popular commodity back then. Apples, peaches, and pears were sliced and spread out to dry on a flat surface in the sun. Sheets of galvanized tin were sometimes used, quite often the low near-flat roof of a chicken house. Fried apple or peach pies were real delicacies for the kids, either at mealtime, for school lunches, or as after-school snacks. You are probably thinking, "How sanitary and healthy was fruit dried on an open and not-so-clean tin roof with birds and flies all around?" Well, I will allow you to answer that question, but those fried pies sure were delicious, and we never worried about how sanitary they were.

Butchering hogs was another significant task best performed by two families. The only meat we ate was chickens we raised, pork we slaughtered, wild birds and game we killed, and fish we caught, so hog-killing time at the first real cold spell each winter was a big event. But, it was not the cleanest job on the farm.

Someone with an accurate aim and a steady hand, usually my father, shot the hog with a 22 rifle. Occasionally, the first shot did not kill him, so a second shot was necessary. Next, someone stuck the hog in the heart with a long butcher knife to "bleed" him. The men then dragged the hog or hauled it in a wagon to the location where it was to be butchered. Weak stomachs and butchering hogs did not mix well.

The men placed a huge metal drum into a large hole dug at an angle. They heated water to a boil in a cast iron wash pot and poured it into the drum. We lowered one end of the hog into the drum of boiling water, pulled it out of the water, and scraped off its hair using sharp butcher knives. We repeated the process until all the hair was scraped off. Shaving a hog was obviously a dirty and smelly undertaking. The men hung the scraped hog by its back legs, split it open, and gutted it. They then placed the hog on a large table and cut it into sections. Portions of the hog, such as the hams, were smoke-cured in a smoke house, whereas other portions were cut up and packed with salt in a large wooden box for preservation. We also cut up parts of the hog and ground them into sausage using a hand-cranked meat grinder.

Butchering A Hog

One of the women's jobs during hog butchering was cleaning the intestines, or chitterlings, called "chitlins" back then. The women cooked the chitlins and we ate them, or they were used to stuff sausage for curing in the smoke house. Farmers did not waste any of the hog except the hide, hair, and squeal. People ate the hog's head, tongue, feet, and other comely parts in some form (for example, as sausage or hog's head cheese) or boiled them in the cast iron wash pot to produce lard for cooking. A by-product of making lard was cracklings, a crisp residue used in cooking, especially in crackling cornbread. One hog-killing time stands out in my memory. Uncle Charlie's pig pen was quite a distance from his house, so he hauled the dead hog in a horse-drawn wagon to our house for butchering. The horses apparently smelled the blood, panicked, and ran away out of control. That hog got a wild and bumpy ride through the rough pasture before the horses were brought under control.

A few farmers butchered young steers occasionally to provide beef for their families, and usually neighboring families. Daddy never butchered a steer, so I am not familiar with that process. Farm folks in the twenties and thirties were resourceful and creative. They ate what they raised for the most part, and very little food was wasted. They fed all food scraps and leftovers to the cats, dogs, chickens, or pigs. A staple in all kitchens was a "slop bucket," used to collect scraps and leftovers for the pigs. Peelings and trimmings from fruits and vegetables were fed to the chickens or pigs; everything was "recycled" back then.

Families often got together on holidays or special occasions. Feasting on homemade ice cream on the Fourth of July was a tradition with the Hill family. The ladies prepared the ice cream mix, some with fresh peaches, and the men finished the job using hand-cranked freezers. The kids argued about who would sit on the cold freezers to hold them down, and we could hardly wait until the ice cream was firm enough to eat. I continued that Fourth of July tradition with my own family. We sat on our patio each Fourth of July, ate hand-cranked ice cream, and watched the fireworks at a nearby high school stadium.

I was an only child, so I did not have brothers and sisters to play with; I had to entertain myself a significant portion of the time. Two of my cousins, Doyle and Bonnie, lived a little ways down the road from us, however, and we spent a lot of time together. They were the nearest thing I had to a brother or sister, and we became very close during our adolescent years. Like all farm kids, we had limited play time during the farming season, but Fall and Winter brought us ample free time. We spent many happy hours outside playing hide-and-seek, tag, baseball, jump rope, marbles, mumble-peg, tree-climbing, cowboys and Indians, and various other games.

Farm kids had a wide choice of indoor activities in cold or rainy weather. We did not have television, video games, cell phones, CD players, an abundance of store-bought toys, or any high-tech gadgets, but we found fun games to play. We played dominoes or shoot-the-moon a lot, and Uncle Charlie joined us quite often for a game of 42. Other favorite indoor activities were checkers, jacks, bingo, Chinese checkers, reading, jigsaw puzzles, and (shudder) playing with dolls. Needless to say, we also got into a lot of mischief; we were no different from most kids our ages. Most women and a lot of men dipped snuff in those days, and of course we had to try it. I remember one time in particular we sneaked some of the adults' snuff and hid behind the barn to dip it. I must have swallowed some snuff because I became very sick; I thought I would die. I don't think I dipped any more snuff after that.

Seventy years ago, people were not aware of the potential risks involved with use of tobacco products. A vast majority of men smoked, chewed tobacco, or dipped snuff, and a lot of women dipped snuff. I remember finding a small tree branch, cutting off a three-inch section, and chewing the end to soften it and thus make a snuff brush for Grandma Hill; she could not chew the brush herself because of bad teeth. Society frowned on women who smoked, whereas dipping snuff was acceptable. I often heard my parents' generation castigate some young "hussy" for smoking while dipping snuff themselves. Men bought bulk tobacco in large cans and rolled their own cigarettes; "ready-rolls" were too expensive. Daddy carried his tobacco, paper, and matches in a small Prince Albert can to keep them dry, and he refilled his small tin from a large Prince Albert can. Most boys started smoking in their teens and continued that harmful habit into adulthood.

I smoked tobacco a few times as a youngster, but I never inhaled, so I did not develop that nasty habit. My cousins and I tried quite a few tobacco substitutes. We sneaked around and smoked dried corn silks; we smoked small sections of dried weeds called rabbit weeds; and we smoked pieces of dried grapevine. Of the three, dried grapevine was our favorite, but grapevine smoke really burned our mouths. I did not smoke in my adult years, so I never suffered from nicotine addiction as most of my peers did.

I enjoyed overnight visits with a few cousins at times. Edgar, Harold, Kenneth, Wayne, and I spent occasional nights together, and sometimes the visits were for several days. Those were memorable times with my cousins. One of my favorite older cousins was Eva, Grandma Hill's oldest grandchild; she was the same age as Mother. Eva and her husband, Elmer, lived near Louisiana at the time, but they visited Grandma Hill each Sunday. They always brought me the Sunday funny papers, a treat I eagerly looked forward to. I could not wait to see what was happening to Tarzan, Li'l Abner, Blondie and Dagwood, Buck Rogers, Dick Tracy, Alley Oop, Little Orphan Annie, Mutt and Jeff, and all the other funny paper heroes. I spent an enjoyable week with Eva and Elmer one time before Elmer was called to serve in the war.

I remember two humorous incidents when I visited Eva. She lived in Atlanta while Elmer was away in the military, and Doyle and I visited her there. She had both an outhouse and an indoor toilet. Doyle and I had never used an indoor toilet, so we used the outhouse while we were there, except for one time. We decided to try the commode and came to the conclusion to push the little lever down when we were finished. The sudden noise and rush of water scared us; we thought we had broken the commode. That is two real country bumpkins for you.

Another time, Edgar and I visited Eva and Elmer in Beaumont just before I enlisted in the Air Force; that was my last fling before leaving for basic training. Eva took us next door and introduced us to two pretty girls, the Ayo twins. We were there only a few minutes when all of a sudden a man's legs came crashing through the ceiling above us. We were startled but rushed to help him down. Mr. Ayo was up in the attic doing some work, or perhaps eavesdropping on his daughters, when he fell through the ceiling sheetrock. We did have a lot of fun though with Betty and Beverly on that vacation; I wrote to Betty a few times while in the Air Force, and I met her brother at Keesler Air Force Base in Mississippi.

A group of cousins gathered at my house a lot on Sunday afternoons for various games. I hung a basketball goal on the side of our barn and marked off a makeshift basketball half-court. An older cousin, Vaudine, and her husband, Clifton, gave me a basketball, so I thought I was in hog's heaven. I spent many contented hours alone shooting goals on that dirt court, and my cousins and I played basketball there quite often. We also played baseball in our pasture, and we played football occasionally, with our football being burlap bags wound tightly and tied in the general shape of a football. We had great difficulty passing that burlap bag football, and kicking it was really a joke. Money was not available to purchase sports equipment, so we improvised as best we could.

Kids in the thirties loved to chew gum, but hardly ever got to do so; we simply did not have money to buy gum. But, we did not give up. Youngsters found their chewing gum in the woods. A lot of sweet gum trees gave off sap, and that sap hardened to produce chunks of "gum." I chewed many chunks of gum from sweet gum trees in my adolescent years. I never tried it, but one of my cousins tells me she mixed sweet gum tree sap with berries from a vine to produce bubblegum. Parents, when your precious little one asks for gum, take him or her into the woods and find a sweet gum tree. Another of my cousins, Helen, relates how her mother set her hair using sugar water; she did not know if her mother used something with the sugar water or not. Try it ladies and see how it works.

Harold, a cousin, reminds me of a funny incident during one of my visits with him. We went to see one of his cousins,

Lawrence, who lived nearby. Lawrence convinced Harold and me that a lot of the rocks around his house contained gold, and he even selected those rocks with gold streaks. Harold and I filled our pockets with those gold rocks; we thought we were rich. You can imagine how letdown and stupid we felt when we realized we had been duped. We were just two gullible hicks from the sticks.

Harold's father, Uncle Leonard, claimed the only shower in the area. He was one of the few farmers who had a manual pump in his water well, and he ran a line from the pump to an elevated barrel in his back yard. He then attached a shower outlet to the bottom of the barrel. He pumped water into the barrel, and presto, he could stand under the shower outlet and take a shower. Harold tells me one of his chores on the farm was to pump water into the shower barrel.

My cousins and I often walked about one-half mile to a neighbor's farm to go swimming in his stock pond. We invariably stopped by Mr. Upchurch's house to ask permission to swim in his pond, and we sometimes visited with him and his family a few minutes. Folks back then were friendly and neighborly. None of us owned bathing suits and we did not wear underwear, so we always went skinny-dipping, the norm at the time. Mr. Upchurch's pond was a short distance from his house, but we cavorted around in the water, on the bank, and on the dam in our birthday suits. I am sure they saw us but he never complained about it; it was probably a big joke with them.

All farm youngsters had dogs when I was growing up, but we were not always kind to them. My cousins and I found huge wasp nests around our barn and chicken house. We threw rocks and corn cobs at the nests to knock them down, and when we hit a nest, the wasps swarmed after anything nearby, including us. We often lured one of the dogs near a low-hanging nest, threw a rock at the nest, and watched the wasps chase the dog. We also caught white-headed bumblebees, not the black-headed ones because they stung, and tied them to short pieces of string. We held a bumblebee tightly so it could not buzz and looped the string around a dog's neck, with the bumblebee a few inches behind the dog's head. We then let go of the bumblebee, and when it started buzzing, the dog went crazy. Those are just two of the mean things we did to our pets.

A group of neighbor boys met on some Saturday afternoons at Anti for a baseball game near the Antioch Baptist Church. The Anti pasture we played in was about one and one-half miles from my house. We worked long hours on the farm from Monday through Saturday morning, walked to Anti, played baseball several hours, and walked home. Folks in the thirties worked extremely hard but found time for fun and recreation. And, we did not have soccer moms, scout leaders, and car pools to chauffeur us to the various activities; we hoofed it. A diet heavy in vegetables, physical farm work, extensive walking, and abundant exercise minimized the incidence of obesity in the twenties and thirties. Today's society should hearken back to those healthy practices.

Grandma Hill and Grandpa Hill, who died in 1926 before I was born, raised their family in the Baptist faith, whereas Mama Brown and Daddy Brown practiced the Mormon religion. Most of the extended Hill family worshiped in Missionary Baptist Churches, now called Southern Baptist. But one of my uncles was a Primitive Baptist (Hard-shell Baptist) pastor for many years, and several cousins converted to the Pentecostal faith, with one becoming a lifetime pastor. One thing has not changed in the last seventy years. People argued about religion in the thirties as they do today. I recall a group of Hill cousins sitting around on Sunday afternoons with two or three of them arguing about some Biblical issue. I do not remember the specific topics, but the arguments usually involved differences between Baptist and Pentecostal beliefs.

Divorce is a common and widely accepted phenomenon in today's society. Couples rarely divorced in my generation, and a stigma was attached to those who did, but divorce was virtually unheard of in my parents' generation. A few folks, predominately men, did seek affection outside of their marriages, but such infidelity was generally the result of some underlying problem, typically alcoholism. Marriage was considered to be a lifelong relationship, and most couples honored that commitment. A vast majority of marriages survived even with the extended

27

deployment of millions of husbands in World War II. I am sure most married couples experienced turbulence in their marital life back then, as married folks do now, but they just worked through it. And, marriage counseling was unheard of in those days. The high divorce rate of today is, I believe, an indication of the culture of self-centeredness and self-gratification which has gradually permeated our society over the last sixty years.

Folks were poor in the twenties and thirties, they faced tremendous economic difficulties, and they struggled to survive, yet they maintained stable families. How could that be? Perhaps people back then did not realize their plight because everyone was in the same boat. Few of them acquired much of an education, so they did not harbor lofty aspirations and dreams for their lives as people do today; they did not have to deal with career and economic disappointments. In addition, most rural folks shared common interests and similar professions, so they were content with their particular stations in life. They did not seek greener pastures on the other side of the fence. The bottom line is that people were happy and content, a basic requirement for a stable family.

3.

Our Houses

Rural folks lived in unpainted wood frame houses when I was growing up. Their houses were not fancy, but they were sturdy. A house was normally supported by brick or concrete blocks, with a crawl space beneath the floor. The blocks were only a few inches high on the upper side of sloping house plots and up to three or four feet high on the lower side, providing a convenient shelter for pets and a place for kids to play. The front porch of our house was close to the ground, whereas the back porch was about three feet off the ground. The flooring in a majority of houses utilized finished boards, but the outer walls were built quite often with unfinished lumber. A typical house incorporated vertical 12-inch boards on the outside walls with 4-inch boards covering the cracks, but some houses were constructed with horizontal boards on the outer walls.

A lot of the roofs incorporated wood shingles, but others were constructed using galvanized tin to reduce cost. Steady rain on a tin roof was a soothing sound, but hail or sleet was quite loud. A majority of farm houses were finished with wood ceilings and wood inside walls, but a few had no inner walls at all opposite exterior walls, resulting in frigid inside temperatures on cold winter nights. Very few houses contained ceiling or wall insulation in the twenties and thirties, and most of the bedrooms were unheated. Three or four heavy quilts on each bed kept people warm during cold weather. Everyone made sure all fires in fireplaces and wood-burning heaters died out before bedtime, for safety reasons, so the entire house was very cold by morning. We got out of bed and dressed in a cold room in the winter time. Daddy slept in only his underwear, and firewood for the fireplace was stored in a box on the front porch. He got out of bed each winter morning, walked out to the porch in his underwear to get wood, made a fire in the living room fireplace, and then dressed in his cold bedroom. Guys, how would you like to do that each winter morning rather than crawl out of bed to quickly change the thermostat and then jump back in bed?

The size and layout of houses depended on family size. Larger families required bigger kitchen/dining areas and a larger number of bedrooms. Quite a few houses, especially the smaller ones, featured hallways through the center of the dwellings. The kitchen and combination bedroom/living area were located on one side of the hallway, with other bedrooms on the opposite side. Occasionally, a house featured two fireplaces, one in the living area and one in a bedroom across the hallway. That was the layout of the house in which I was born. The second house I lived in prior to graduating from high school was heated only by a wood-burning heater in the living room, and the house did not have a hallway.

Virtually all farm houses included huge front porches, usually extending all the way across the front of the house, and large back porches near the kitchens. Folks sat on the front porch in the evening to get away from the hot stuffy temperature inside and to greet neighbors who happened to pass by. Neighbors who passed by sometimes stopped to chat awhile with those on the front porch. The back porch was an ideal place to sit and shell peas or beans in hot weather. A wash stand on the back porch held a bucket of drinking water and a dipper and provided a place to wash hands before a meal. A large No. 2 wash tub on the back porch facilitated bathing after dark.

Daddy Brown on the Front Porch

Our second house incorporated a relatively small back porch, so our "bath tub" was placed on the ground adjacent to the back steps. All three of us bathed after dark in the same tub of water; I went first, Mother was second, and Daddy was last. Mother and I finished our baths one night and went to visit Uncle Charlie and his family down the road, leaving Daddy in the No. 2 tub. A neighbor, Mrs. Blalock, stopped by for a visit. She called us but did not receive an answer. Mrs. Blalock heard noises from the back of the house, so she walked around to the back yard and caught Daddy in the bath tub. I am sure she was as startled as he was. Our bath tub was relocated to one of the bedrooms in cold weather, but our daily baths were infrequent in the winter time. After all, we did not sweat, so we did not "need" a bath very often.

A multi-purpose barn was essential for all farms, oftentimes larger than the dwelling. Several stalls, some enclosed and others not, provided feed and shelter for cows, mules, and horses and a place to milk the cows. Rooms, or cribs, provided storage for corn, cotton seed, fertilize, and other products. Each crib contained a small access door to the outside, as well as a larger door to a walkway on the inside of the barn. A hay loft in the attic supplied ample storage space for corn tops, peanut vines, and other types of hay for the livestock. Access to the hay loft was through a large door at one end of the barn. A wagon load of hay parked under the access door enabled Daddy to toss the hay into the loft. My job was to move the hay to the interior of the loft, an extremely hot task in the summer season.

One of my favorite pastimes in cold or rainy weather was picking peanuts off the vines in the hay loft, but I often scared off big rats seeking those same peanuts. We parched the peanuts in a bread pan in the oven of our wood-burning cook stove to provide delicious treats for the entire family. Those were the kinds of simple but pleasant activities which interrupted the drudgery of farm life and brought joy to farm kids. Killing rats in the barn was another popular pastime for my cousins and me. One of us occupied each crib, armed with a large club and a dog. We stirred up the corn, making a lot of noise in the process, to chase the rats out into the open where the dogs killed a lot of them, and we clubbed a few more to death. The barn always contained an ample supply of rats for that game. The rats also attracted large black snakes, referred to as chicken snakes, so we occasionally encountered those snakes as we shucked corn for the horses and pigs. Farm kids experienced all kinds of surprises, a few pleasant but most not so pleasant.

Most barns included attached sheds for wagons, whereas other farms utilized separate wagon sheds. A few farms also featured stand-alone potato houses. We did not have a potato house, so I did not learn a lot about them, but I did see one on my uncle's farm. It was a low building constructed with thick clay, or dirt, walls to provide an insulated storage place for either sweet potatoes (yams) or Irish potatoes (spuds). The insulated house kept potatoes cool in warm weather and warm in cold weather. The potato house functioned as somewhat of a basement, and it was similar to a storm cellar built for protection from tornados.

A staple for all farms was a chicken house, sometimes quite large. A majority of farmers kept a hundred or more chickens to provide an ample supply of eggs, as well as meat for Sunday dinner. Like Mother, a lot of ladies crated eggs and sold them to grocery stores or individuals in Queen City or Atlanta. City folks liked fresh eggs delivered directly from the farm. Mother also sold milk, butter, and cream in Queen City and Atlanta. Income from the sale of those products, together with income from sale of fresh vegetables at times, supplemented the meager income earned from the cotton crop. Such extra income was an absolute necessity for farmers during those hard times.

Chicken houses were low flat buildings with tin roofs. Rows of roosts inside provided a secure place for chickens to settle down at night, and feed and water were kept in either the chicken house or in a pen outside. A large number of farmers allowed the chickens to roam free around the yard, but others kept them in a large pen around the chicken house. A few chickens always tried to roost in trees or bushes outside the chicken house, so a daily chore at dusk was to run those wayward chickens into their house. Any chicken left outside the chicken house at night was an easy meal for raccoons, opossums (or "possums"), and other animals. Cleaning chicken droppings from underneath the roosts was a smelly and dirty task, but that chicken poop was an excellent fertilize for flowers and vegetables.

A multi-purpose smoke house was another staple for a farm. The size of the smoke house was determined by the number of functions it provided and the number of people in the family. Farmers smoke-cured hams, sausage, and other meats by hanging them over a hickory wood fire. The smoke house usually contained a large wooden box in which other meats were packed in salt for preservation. A lot of smoke houses also incorporated extensive shelving to accommodate storage of several hundred jars of canned fruits, vegetables, preserves, and jellies. Farmers often used the smoke house for storage of feed for the chickens and livestock as well, so a smoke house was an important and sometimes sizeable structure on a farm.

An indoor toilet was a convenience of the future where I grew up, so an outhouse was essential. The outhouse was always located at some distance from the dwelling for obvious reasons. A small wood structure with a tin roof incorporated a flat bench-like surface inside, about fifteen inches from the floor. One or two round holes, for either a one-seater or a two-seater, respectively, provided "seats" in the flat surface. A deep hole dug underneath the seats provided waste disposal, and Sears & Roebuck catalogues served as paper goods. The women and girls frequented the outhouse, whereas the men and boy's favorite spot was behind the barn, and corn cobs served as paper goods for them. A mean trick on Halloween was tipping over a farmer's outhouse, something I never did of course.

Farmhouses did not have lawns in the twenties and thirties; we had yards instead. A large number of farms featured front yards void of grass and weeds, but adorned with an abundance of flowers. The women and children hoed away any grass and weeds found in the yard and carefully cultivated all kinds of flowers and flowering bushes. Shrubs and greenery were not "in things" with Mother's generation. Some flowers were planted in beds, but others were just randomly placed around the yard. Fertilize for the yard was produced by chickens and livestock, and I do not recall serious problems with insects or drought.

Furniture for farm homes was practical and plain back then, a lot of it homemade. Each kitchen contained a wood-burning cook stove, a plain wood table with either benches or straight chairs, and a pie safe, just the bare essentials. The chairs were either cane-bottom or hide-bottom, with the hide being dried animal skins. Wash stands stood on the back porches of most houses, but they were located in the kitchens in others. A stove wood box occupied a corner behind the cook stove, and an oil tablecloth sometimes graced the dining table. My house today contains relics of that time period, passed down to me by Mother. I have her pie safe, wash stand, and two straight chairs.

Christine, one of my cousins, has an interesting story about her and Clyde's first chairs. They had no furniture when they married, so various family members gave them furniture items. Uncle Leonard contributed two chairs, both with their bottoms missing. Clyde found enough cowhide, the usual chair bottom material, for one of the chairs, but he had to use goat hide on the other one. As everyone is well aware, a wet goat puts out a terrible odor, so that goat hide chair did not smell very good in damp weather.

Rocking chairs were popular in the twenties and thirties, so most living rooms contained two or three rockers and perhaps some straight chairs. A few living rooms featured sofa chairs, but most contained one or more beds. A table holding a coal oil lamp was a fixture in each living area, and a majority of living rooms included a battery-powered radio, analogous to a television set today. The radios were either floor-standing consoles or large bulky table models, and the rectangular batteries were huge and heavy. The antenna, or aerial, for the radio was a wire strung between two tall poles located near the house. I remember all the men and boys gathered around the radio listening to boxing matches, especially Joe Louis' fights, with his first fight with Billy Conn being the most memorable one. The entire family looked forward to the Grand Ole Opry broadcast from Nashville each Saturday night; I recently had the privilege of visiting the historic Ryman Auditorium where those broadcasts originated. And of course, a lot of the ladies listened faithfully to the weekday soap operas, including Our Gal Sunday, Young Dr. Malone, The Guiding Light, and others

Bedrooms were furnished with one or more double beds, usually with iron bedsteads, each holding a set of springs and one or two plain cotton-filled mattresses. A cushy feather mattress was often added in cold weather for greater warmth. A wardrobe and chest of drawers in each bedroom provided storage for the few clothes people owned, and one or two chairs were often included in a bedroom as well. Three or four family members sometimes shared a single bedroom, so little room was available for anything other than the beds. Farm folks spent a lot of time on the front porch, so rocking chairs and perhaps straight chairs were kept there. Homes in the twenties and thirties were furnished with just the bare essentials, nothing fancy.

Quilting was a popular activity with the ladies, necessitated by the need for heavy covers on the beds during cold winters. Quilting frames were suspended from the ceilings in most living areas; the frames were lowered and raised as needed. The ladies first pieced the individual squares, and then they sewed the squares together with backing and a border to form the entire quilt. The quilt was then attached to the frame and the ladies sat around the frame and completed the job. Most houses included large wooden boxes to store an abundant supply of quilts when they were not needed on the beds. My daughter, grandchildren, and I have a large number of homemade quilts passed down to me by Mother and Grandma Hill, and some of those quilts are beautiful works of art.

We did not have electricity in our community when I was growing up, so we relied on inexpensive coal oil lamps for light. An advanced, or brighter, version of coal oil lamps was the Aladdin Lamp, and we had one of those brighter models. I did my reading and homework through high school by the light of those coal oil lamps and sunshine, and Mother did her sewing and quilting by lamp light. The light from a coal oil lamp was dim, but we made do with what we had.

Our source of water was a well thirty to fifty feet deep and four to five feet in diameter, from which we drew water in a galvanized bucket. A rope attached to the bucket and run through a pulley mounted above the well enabled us to draw water manually. We thus obtained water manually for drinking, cooking, hand washing, bathing, and laundry, in addition to water for pets, chickens, and livestock. Water from those wells was very cold and refreshing, and it was void of the normal bad taste and odor of a lot of city water back then.

A few people utilized hand pumps mounted over the wells, but we drew water the old fashion way, with a bucket. Those uncovered wells did present a problem, however. Occasionally, a small animal, usually a rat, fell into the well, and after a few days the water began to smell. When that occurred, we drew the well down very low and removed the culprit, but that was quite a task. Two or three men took turns drawing water bucket-by-bucket as rapidly as they could to lower the water level in the well. The men had to draw water out of the well faster than it ran in to lower the water level. At some point, the animal causing the odor showed up in a bucket of water. They drew the well down as low as possible and then allowed it to fill back up. The water was pure again. On rare occasions, someone was lowered into the well to clean it out and make needed repairs.

We did not have electricity, so food storage and preservation was a concern, especially for folks who did not have iceboxes. Ice was delivered once or twice a week to people who had iceboxes and could afford it, and those iceboxes facilitated limited storage of perishable food such as milk and butter. Space was very limited in an icebox, however, so most folks kept their milk, butter, and other perishable food cold by lowering it in buckets into the well. Ice was kept primarily for use in iced tea at meal times. Our first icebox was a wooden box wrapped in wet burlap bags for insulation and buried under our back porch. That make-shift icebox kept ice for two or three days, so we enjoyed iced tea with meals a few times a week.

Most families owned a treadle type sewing machine which was used to make virtually all the women's and girl's clothing. Dress patterns were in great demand, and the ladies traded them back and forth with one another. Shopping for a new dress in the thirties was a unique experience. Chicken feed came in cotton print sacks in a variety of patterns. I often watched Mother search through stacks of chicken feed in the hardware store to find enough sacks with the same pattern to make a dress. She was thrilled when she found a print pattern she really liked. Mother could hardly wait until the chicken feed was used up and she could make a new dress. All the women we knew shopped for dresses the same way. Ladies, how would you like to do your shopping for a new dress in a feed store? Or girls, how would you like to wear a feed sack dress on a date?

Ironing was also a little different back then. Ladies washed shirts, khaki pants, dresses, and other items and starched them stiff. They sprinkled the starched clothes and ironed them using solid cast-iron irons. Women heated irons on either the wood-burning cook stove or a bed of hot coals in the fireplace. They used one iron to press clothes while another iron was being heated, and then they exchanged the two irons. Again ladies, how would you like to do your ironing that way?

The dwelling, furnishings, barn, and associated structures described herein are the ones in which I lived, worked, and played, but they are representative of those used by my peers. Some people's houses and structures were larger and perhaps a little nicer than those of their neighbors, depending on a family's size and economic means. Particular layouts and furnishings varied somewhat, but all of us lived comparable lives. A few folks were a little better off economically than others, but all of us were poor, and our lifestyles reflected that common thread.

4.

Farming in the Thirties

F armers in the twenties and thirties did not have the advanced tractors and mechanized disks, plows, bedders and planters, combines, cotton pickers and strippers, corn pickers and shellers, herbicide and fertilize applicators, defoliant applicators, and other farm equipment of today. Neither did they have genetically engineered cotton and corn nor advanced fertilize and herbicides to control insects and increase yields. Modern farm technology drastically changed the farming landscape across America over the last seventy years. The manual small-family farms of the thirties were replaced with the much larger mechanized commercial farms of today. Small family farms are very rare today.

I grew up on a traditional family farm in East Texas, very much like thousands of family farms across the South. Ours was a two-horse farm, large enough to support a family of four or less, but small enough to facilitate farming with two horses or mules. Our 50-acre spread included acreage for corn, cotton, and various other commodities, a pasture for livestock, a small tract of timber, and a typical rural home site. We did all planting, cultivation, and harvesting manually with the aid of horse-drawn farm equipment. Daddy and I did the plowing with a horse and a mule, and Mother helped with the other farm tasks. Cotton was our money crop; corn provided feed for the chickens and livestock; and we raised watermelons, ribbon cane, peanuts, cantaloupes, potatoes, various fruits, and all kinds of vegetables for our own consumption.

I do not remember the first time I plowed, but I am sure I was no more than nine years of age at the time. I do recall walking behind the plow with my head just slightly above the plow handles and having to reach up to hold the handles. I had difficulty turning the plow around at the end of rows; I was not big enough and strong enough to swing the plow around as quickly as the horse made the turn to the next row. I also helped Daddy hoe cotton and corn and harvest our crops as far back as I can remember. I loved to work in the fields, so I started helping out at a very young age. I helped with farm chores around the house as far back as I recollect as well.

We lived on a tenant farm, so the owner shared the costs of seeds and fertilize, received one-third of the corn harvest, and claimed one-fourth of the proceeds from sale of the cotton harvest. The owner also shared the cost of insecticides if needed. Ours was the standard arrangement for tenant farms during that time period. Additional income received from sale of livestock, dairy products, eggs, fruits, or vegetables supplemented our cotton harvest earnings, and the farm owner kept the proceeds from timber sales.

There was one exception to the owner's income from sale of timber. He sold the pine timber off our farm during my junior year in high school, when I was only thirteen years old. The owner allowed, and even encouraged, me to cut up the residual tree tops into pulp wood (for paper mills), and he let me keep the proceeds from sale of that pulp wood. I worked hard throughout the summer before my senior year, cutting fifty pens (stacks) of pulp wood, and Daddy sold it to a trucker for one dollar per pen. That fifty dollars was sufficient for me to buy school clothes for the year, with money left over to spend throughout the school year. Cutting and stacking pulp wood was hard work for a thirteen year old boy, but fifty dollars was a lot of money for a farm boy back then. And, I was thrilled to make that dollar per day; I felt rich.

Cotton and corn crops consumed a majority of our farm acreage, split about fifty-fifty between the two. Cotton was harvested and sold to earn the family income, whereas the corn harvest provided feed for livestock and chickens. We alternated corn and cotton on each field or farm section every year; rotation of crops maximized productivity of the land. We planted watermelons, cantaloupes, peas, peanuts, ribbon cane, sweet potatoes, Irish potatoes, and other vegetables in smaller sections of the farm.

We disked the fields in early spring and broke them up (turned them over to loosen and aerate the soil) using a Kelly Turning Plow. That was heavy-duty work for a horse or mule because the turning plow turned over several inches of firm topsoil each pass across the field. We used a middle buster, a plow which turned the soil over to both sides, to lay out slightly raised rows of dirt. A fertilize spreader deposited commercial fertilize down each row to ready the field for planting. Farmers planted corn in late March most of the time, and cotton planting followed by about a month, depending on the weather.

We dropped grains of corn by hand about two feet apart, much farther apart than the genetically engineered corn planted today. Corn yield per acre was thus substantially lower in the thirties, compared to the yields achieved today using advanced fertilize and hybrid seeds. In addition, farmers in that time period did not plant one type of corn for human consumption and another for animal feed. People, horses and mules, pigs, and chickens ate the same corn, except for sweet corn planted by a few farmers in vegetable gardens. When the corn plants were two to three inches high, we replanted missing spots, those where the grains did not germinate, by hand using a hoe.

We cultivated, or plowed, the corn using a Georgia Stock Plow, a popular lightweight plow featuring an interchangeable wing-like "sweep." Sweeps of different lengths enabled us to control the amount of soil moved around the corn stalks; longer sweeps moved more dirt and thus raised the row as the corn plants grew. We dropped additional fertilize, normally cotton seed meal, by hand near each corn plant prior to one of the cultivation cycles. We hoed weeds and grass from the corn rows by hand. We made the final plowing pass on the corn with the Kelly Turning Plow which moved more soil around the corn stalks. We then waited for the corn crop to produce.

A One-Horse Plow

Two long wooden handles about two feet apart extended behind a plow, and a horizontal crosspiece connected the handles approximately a foot from their ends. The driver of the plow walked behind the plow between the two handles. The plow occasionally hit a buried root, bringing the plow to a sudden stop, and the driver walked into the horizontal crosspiece, not a pleasant experience. The Georgia Stock sweep sometimes hit a root from one side, causing the plow handles to swing sharply to the right or left and into the side of the driver. Now that smarted. I remember being doubled over in pain after a plow handle poked me in the side or ribs.

The maturing corn stalks put on tassels first, and then tiny ears of corn with silks began to appear. When the ears of corn were mature, but before the stalks began to turn brown, we cut the tops of the stalks off just above the top ears using a sharp knife. The sun dried the corn tops, and we gathered them up and hauled them to the barn in a wagon. Daddy tossed the dried corn tops into the hay loft, I carried them back into the loft, and we had feed for horses, mules, and cattle in the winter. Kids enjoyed riding on top of the loads of corn top hay on the way from the field to the barn, and occasionally one of us got too close to the edge and fell off the wagon.

The uncut bottom portions of the corn stalks, the portions holding the ears of corn, turned brown and died, and the ears of corn on them turned brown and dried as well. The corn was ready to harvest. Corn harvesting was usually a joint effort by Uncle

Charlie, Doyle, Daddy, and me. We drove a wagon down a corn row, stopping every few feet. All of us pulled corn by hand and tossed it into the wagon bed. When all the corn within range of the wagon was pulled, we moved the wagon a little farther down the corn row. We repeated that cycle until the wagon was loaded, and we hauled the harvested corn to the barn and parked the wagon underneath the raised access door to the corn crib. Large shovels enabled us to toss the corn through the access door into the crib, and we then returned to the corn field for another load. My job in corn harvesting was to pull corn from the "down row," the row of corn run over by the wagon.

Pulling Corn

Raising cotton was a little more complicated and time consuming, compared to raising corn. A Georgia Stock opened a furrow down a row, and a cotton seed planter dropped seeds in the furrow at a selected spacing of the seeds. Daddy plowed the furrow, leaving me to operate the seed planter. I had no problem keeping the planter in the furrow going down a row, but turning the heavy planter around at the end of a row was a challenge. A plow horse or mule was trained to make a sharp turn at the end of one row and start immediately back down an adjacent row, and our animals were very good at what they were trained to do. The cotton seed planter was far too heavy for a young lad like me to swing it around to the start of a new row. So, Daddy turned his plow around to a new row, stopped his mule, and turned the planter around for me to the start of the new row. We then proceeded to the other end of the field and repeated the process.

We plowed the cotton plants in much the same manner as corn, but hoeing grass and weeds from cotton rows was more time consuming. Plowing young cotton plants with the Georgia Stock was also tricky; dirt shoved by the plow sweep often pushed the tender plants down or covered them up. I developed a knack for straightening most plants with my bare foot without stopping, but I sometimes had to stop the horse and uncover the plants. A good plow horse obeyed four commands: Whoa, or stop; Gee, or turn right; Haw, or turn left; and Get up, or move forward. Reins connected to a bit in the horse's mouth and tied to the ends of a rope looped around the driver's waist, or to two ropes with the other ends looped around the driver's wrists, provided a means of controlling the animal. A large horse connected to a rope looped around a little guy like me was probably a strange sight, but I felt I was in control.

The cotton plants were fragile and planted close together, so hoeing grass and weeds out of the row was tedious work, requiring a great amount of patience. Some areas of the fields were infested with Bermuda grass or Johnson grass, and those areas were particularly troublesome. We exercised extreme care in hoeing the grass without damaging or destroying the cotton plants. We referred to that hoeing process as chopping cotton, and it had to be repeated two or three times as the cotton plants grew. Daddy hired a few workers, usually neighbor ladies, to help us chop cotton. Some of the workers were much faster than others, but Daddy paid them all the same wages. He did not want to cheat anyone out of any money, a trait he instilled in me.

I remember one couple in particular who helped us chop cotton, and they often helped us do other farm tasks. They were an unusual pair, so I will not divulge their real names. Mr. and Mrs. "Smith" lived in a shack back in the woods not far from our house. Their house was very small, with a dirt floor, and their stove pipe exited on the side of the house rather than on the roof.

Wind blew smoke back into the house, so the inside of their house and their skins were dark and dingy due to the smoke. The Smiths did very little farming for themselves; they worked for other folks as much as they could.

Mr. and Mrs. Smith often "dropped in" unannounced on someone around dinner time, expecting an invitation to eat. Note that farmers in the thirties ate breakfast, dinner, and supper, not breakfast, lunch, and dinner; we were not citified. The Smith's dinner visits always included Sundays after church. I remember many occasions when they stopped by our house for Sunday dinner. My parents were very hospitable, so they always welcomed Mr. and Mrs. Smith even though they were not the cleanest folks around and had terrible table manners. Mrs. Smith was a fast worker, whereas Mr. Smith was extremely slow, and he had a speech impediment. She was an odd person. She acted weird and talked irrational at times, and I believe she was eventually committed to a mental institution. They were called insane asylums back then.

Cotton farmers in the thirties faced three common deterrents to a bountiful harvest. Lack of sufficient rain, or too much rain, sometimes reduced the yield per acre; a good yield in those days was one 500-pound bale of cotton per acre. Boll weevils presented a problem then as they do now, but we did not have the effective eradication programs of today. Army worms were another scourge for cotton crops. Boll weevils infected the squares or young bolls, and army worms ate the plants' foliage. Army worms moved from field to field in armies and could destroy a cotton crop in one or two days. We applied insecticides manually with either a duster or a sprayer to combat those pesky insects.

Farmers plowed the cotton fields for the final time and waited for the crop to produce. Squares, blooms, and bolls appeared, and at maturity the bolls opened up to present a white field of cotton ready to harvest. Farmers picked the cotton by hand; we did not have the mechanized pickers and strippers farmers have employed since the sixties. Each of us dragged a large canvas sack by means of a strap across our shoulder, and we picked the cotton from each individual boll and placed it in the sack. We dragged the sack between two rows of cotton and picked from two rows each pass across the field.

Cotton Ready to Pick

Picking Cotton

A dried and open cotton boll had a sharp point on each section of the boll, thus each boll contained a number of stickers. Our fingers turned raw and sometimes bled from those sharp stickers, but we just toughed it out. Pickers carried full sacks to a wagon parked in the field, and Daddy weighed the cotton and poured it into the wagon. Daddy hired extra help to pick cotton, and he paid the workers by the pound picked. Farmers were in the field before sunrise, and they often worked past sundown; those were long days in the spring and summer. We often lit matches to enable us to weigh the last sack of cotton in the evening.

The nearest cotton gin was in Queen City, about ten miles away. Daddy normally hired a neighbor with a truck to haul his cotton to the gin, but I remember once when we hauled it in our wagon. Daddy and I packed our lunches, hitched up the horse and mule to the loaded wagon, and left home well before daylight. A huge vacuum tube at the gin sucked the cotton out of our wagon. We waited for the cotton to be ginned, picked up our cotton seeds resulting from that process, and returned home in our wagon. We arrived home after dark, so it was a long day. Kids loved to play on piles of cotton before it was hauled to the gin, and we played on the piles of cotton seed as well.

Corn and cotton were our primary crops, but we also raised other commodities. All farmers planted sizeable watermelon and cantaloupe patches. We planted Stone Mountain watermelons most of the time, but we also planted other varieties at times, including Black Diamond, Tom Watson, and Cuban Queen. Our watermelon patch was about one-quarter mile from our house, and we lugged a lot of the earliest melons to our house in sacks on our backs. I carried one watermelon at a time, but Daddy often carried two. After a majority of the watermelons and cantaloupes ripened, we hauled them in a wagon to the barn for storage.

We ate a large watermelon every afternoon for a snack. I loved watermelon then, and my taste buds have not changed. I ate the heart from a watermelon half first, and then picked out the seeds and scraped the inside to produce a large amount of juice. I cut a notch in the rind and drank the juice, and boy was it delicious. In later years, I continued that tradition with my daughter and granddaughter. Remember our weird neighbor, Mrs. Smith? She often dropped by during our afternoon watermelon snack, and Mother always invited her to join us. She loved watermelon too, and juice ran down her arms and dripped off her elbows as she ate. Like I said before, Mrs. Smith did not have the best table manners. We also fed watermelons to hogs, chickens, and other livestock. I remember carrying a large watermelon to the pigpen, breaking it open, eating the heart out of it, and feeding the remainder to the pigs. Occasionally, Daddy was able to sell a few watermelons, but the income was minimal.

Sweet potatoes and Irish potatoes were also staples on our farm. Both were harvested the same way. Daddy used a Kelly Turning Plow to turn over the rows of potato plants (Irish potatoes) and potato vines (sweet potatoes), thus loosening the soil around the potatoes and bringing them closer to the surface of the ground. We crawled around on the ground digging potatoes out of the loose dirt with our hands. What would that do to your manicure ladies? We then piled the potatoes into a wagon and hauled them to the barn for storage. Farmers often stored potatoes under beds and under their back porches, all cool dark places. We gleaned the potato patches after the first big rain washed away soil to expose potatoes missed the first time.

Daddy sometimes raised ribbon cane to produce syrup for our own consumption. I do not remember a lot about raising ribbon cane, but I do remember chewing sections of a ribbon cane stalk when it was ready for harvest, and that was a real treat. We cut the ribbon cane stalks and hauled them in a wagon to a nearby neighbor's syrup mill. There, the syrup mill operator ran the ribbon cane through a horse-powered press to squeeze out the juice, caught the juice, and piped it to a large flat rectangular pan over a large fire. He cooked the juice into syrup and transferred it into one-gallon buckets.

As a by-product of syrup making, some folks converted "cane skimmings" from the large syrup pan into some kind of bootleg whiskey. The syrup mill owner, Mr. Upchurch, kept a portion of the syrup as his pay. We ate syrup at most every meal, especially breakfast. We poured our plates full of syrup, mixed in fresh butter, and sopped it with homemade biscuits. That was good eating. A few farmers raised sorghum to produce syrup, but it was not as sweet as ribbon cane syrup.

We had a large fruit orchard with peaches, apples, pears, and plums; we raised all kinds of vegetables; and wild berries were readily available. Farm folks enjoyed fresh fruits, vegetables, and berries in season, and they ate canned produce in the off-season. Mother filled several hundred Mason jars with fruit, vegetables, preserves, and jellies each year, and she canned all of them in a pressure cooker on a wood-burning cook stove in a hot kitchen. Canning was a family job, sometimes including more than one family. The men and boys picked and gathered the vegetables, fruit, and berries. The men and kids shelled, peeled, snapped, shucked, cleaned, and otherwise prepared the produce for canning. The ladies then cooked and canned everything in Mason jars. We were poor, but we had plenty to eat.

Peas were by far the most popular vegetable in our household; we ate fresh peas most every day in season and ate canned peas nearly as often out of season. Daddy often stated that when he died and his blood was drained out it would be mostly pea soup. We always had other vegetables along with peas. Mother made biscuits and cornbread each day, and we ate ribbon cane syrup with almost every meal. Daddy had to have his sliced onions for dinner and supper, and Mother kept a jar of homemade cucumber pickles and a bottle of her pepper sauce on the table. Our diet contained very little meat other than what we raised. We enjoyed fresh pork following hog-killing time, sausage for breakfast quite often, fish occasionally, and perhaps fried chicken for Sunday dinner. Mother baked all kinds of cookies, cakes, muffins, pies, and puddings for dessert, so we ate well.

Miss Manners would not have been pleased with our table etiquette. We used a fork to stick a piece of meat or a slice of tomato for transfer onto our plate, but we ate our food from a spoon. Men poured a cup of hot coffee into a saucer to cool it and then supped it from the saucer. We crumbled crackers or cornbread into soup before we ate it, and we ate with both elbows on the table. We sopped syrup, soup from vegetables, or gravy with a piece of biscuit held in our hand, and a few brave souls attempted to eat peas with a knife. And, "pot liquor" was concocted by crumbling cornbread into soup from turnip greens. Guys, try some of those practices at home and see how your better half reacts.

My family did not own store-bought sheets, pillow cases, towels, or wash cloths. Mother made all those things, plus a lot of other household items and clothing, from fertilize sacks. Fertilize came in white cotton sacks with black letters. Women unraveled those sacks and boiled them through repetitive cycles in an iron wash pot to remove the black letters. They cut up the sacks or sewed them together and hemmed them to produce bed sheets, pillow cases, towels, wash cloths, ladies gowns, slips, underwear, and various other household items. Women also dyed the fertilize sacks to obtain material for quilts and other sewing needs.

Mother did not buy any soap products. She made soap by boiling a mixture of lye and hog fat in the iron wash pot. She cut the cooled soap into bars for use in hand washing, bathing, dish washing, laundry, and mopping and scrubbing floors. Lye soap was powerful stuff, but it was rough on the hands. I did not get a store-bought haircut before I finished high school. Daddy owned a pair of hand clippers, and he cut a lot of our neighbors' hair. Two or three neighbors stopped by almost every Sunday for haircuts, and Daddy never charged them anything. My haircuts were free until I moved away from home, but boy did those hand clippers pull.

We did our laundry manually, using two No. 2 wash tubs, a rub board, and the iron wash pot. Mother heated water in the wash pot and scrubbed the clothes on the rub board in a tub of hot water. She boiled the clothes in the wash pot and we rinsed them in a tub of cold water. Mother then hung the clothes to dry on a clothes line in our yard. My job on laundry day was rinsing, although I occasionally tried my hand on the rub board. There were few tasks on the farm I did not attempt at one time or another.

Mother completed a big pile of laundry one day and hung it out to dry on the clothes line in our yard. I found some mud dirt dauber nests, and for some reason proceeded to throw them at Mother's fresh laundry. She had to rewash some of her laundry to remove the dirt. I knew I was in deep doo-doo, so I crawled under the house. Mother told me to come out, but I told her, "I will if you don't whip me." I do not recall how long I stayed under the house or the final outcome, but Mother most likely gave my behind and legs a good switching with a peach tree limb. Switching was her favorite method of punishing me for my misdeeds, and she resorted to that peach tree limb quite often. But, I never received a switching I did not deserve, and I missed a lot of whippings I should have gotten.

Virtually all parents spanked their children at times when I was growing up. We misbehaved quite often and disobeyed our parents, as youngsters do today, but we understood the meaning of "no." When a parent corrected a child for something bad he or she did, or for disobedience of a rule or instruction, the child knew not to argue, whine, or throw a temper tantrum. Children understood discipline and they respected their parents. And, parents did not need a child psychology book to tell them how to raise their kids. They simply applied the old adage, "Spare the rod and spoil the child."

Perhaps a few parents did go overboard and physically abuse their children, but that was the exception rather than the rule. Kids understood clearly what their parents demanded, and they knew the consequences of disobedience. That early discipline at home carried over into adult years. As students, we respected our teachers, and schools experienced relatively few discipline problems; as employees, we respected and obeyed our superiors in the work place; and as citizens, we obeyed the laws and law enforcers of our land. Unfortunately, the same cannot be said for many of today's youth, our grandchildren. I am convinced that discipline instilled in the home serves a youngster throughout his or her life.

Farm folks had an abundance of daily chores on the farm in addition to the work in the fields. Livestock often failed to come to the barn in the late afternoon, so someone had to find the cattle and horses and drive them in. That was my job at times. We fed all the livestock and chickens and put out water for the hogs and chickens, and that was also my job sometimes. Another daily chore was gathering eggs from numerous hens' nests located around the barn and in the chicken house. Gathering eggs was a regular assignment for me, but it did come with a few risks. The hens were not always happy when I took their eggs, and they let me know it with sharp pecks on the hand. It was also a great shock to peek into a dark nest and find oneself face-to-face with a large black chicken snake; those snakes loved eggs too. Someone had to milk the cows each day, but that was Mother's job a majority of the time; I never learned to milk cows. Pastures were infested with bitter weeds, and the cows ate them, resulting in bitter milk at times.

After the harvest was finished each year, Daddy and I cut a good supply of firewood and stove wood for the winter. We utilized a crosscut saw to cut the wood and split it into smaller pieces if necessary using an axe. We cut the wood from either trees on our farm or from slabs obtained from a nearby sawmill. Daddy "bucked" slabs for the sawmill owner to pay for the slabs. The wood had sufficient time to dry before it was needed in the winter. We found rich "pine knots" or heart pine which we cut into "splinters" to use for starting fires. All farm houses featured huge stacks of fireplace wood and stove wood near the houses.

Times were very difficult in the thirties, and farmers were hard-pressed for funds to pay for planting, cultivating, and harvesting their crops. Many farmers turned to local banks for loans, including Daddy and Uncle Charlie. Those farmers whose credit was good received what were essentially signature loans, or hand-shake loans. The bank loaned a farmer one to two hundred dollars in the spring, and the farmer paid all his farming expenses and lived off that money until harvest time. After harvesting his crops, the farmer paid off all or part of his loan. As far as I know, Daddy was able to repay Atlanta National Bank in full each year, but Uncle Charlie was unable to do so because of his large family. He told Doyle, his son, in 1940 that he was out of debt for the first time in ten years. I am sure many other farmers of that time period were also unable to pay off their crop loans in full each year.

People's attitude toward debt in the thirties was substantially different from young folk's view of debt in today's society. My parents' generation abhorred debt. They paid cash for almost everything they purchased, including farms, new houses, farm equipment, automobiles, and household goods. A few of our neighbors had small charge accounts with grocery stores, drugstores, dry goods stores, and doctors, but a majority of farm folks did without until they could pay cash. My parents were even reluctant to write checks when they had money in the bank to cover the checks. And at that time, a person could write a check on any blank piece of paper, including a brown paper sack. As far as I know, the only debt incurred by my parents each year was that for money to plant, cultivate, and harvest the crops.

Our parents' attitude toward debt rubbed off on my generation, but our society began to change after World War II. Home mortgages and car loans came into prominence, people opened charge accounts in significant numbers in furniture and appliance stores, and credit cards entered the scene. Large numbers of my generation now use credit cards frequently, as I do, but most of us pay off the balances each month. A lot of my peers also have home mortgages, car loans, and other debts, but most of them have incomes and investments sufficient to pay off the loans comfortably. My generation does not abhor debt to the same extent our parents did, but most are careful not to become overextended.

On the other hand, our children and grandchildren view debt from an entirely different perspective. To them, debt is a means of getting what they want rather than what they truly need, and most lack the patience and self-restraint to wait until they can afford it. Too many of our children and grandchildren bought into society's philosophy of, "I want the best, and I must have it now." As a result, they live in expensive houses they cannot afford, drive fancy cars, wear fashion clothing, run up huge student loan debt at the best universities, buy all the latest high-tech gadgets, indulge in expensive hobbies, dine at the finest restaurants, stay in extravagant hotels, travel in fast-paced social circles, and carry huge credit card balances. It seems my generation missed the boat in instilling financial responsibility into our offspring and their kids.

Late fall and winter were seasons for doing odd jobs around the farm. We often repaired the barbed wire fences around our pasture and fields; we cut bushes growing in the fields; and we cleared underbrush from the pasture land. Daddy and I cut a little pulp wood one winter with two of my Brown uncles. When we worked outside during very cold weather, we put on long-johns, two shirts, two pairs of pants, a cap, and heavy gloves, but we froze anyway. We could always find needed work to do in the winter, but we also made time for fun and games, especially during rainy weather. That is when my cousins and I played 42, dominoes, checkers, and other inside games, and I did a lot of reading when I was housebound. I was an avid bookworm until I finished high school. Farm work was hard, but I found it to be an enjoyable and rewarding experience.

5.

A Boy on the Farm

I was an only child during a time period and in a culture wherein most farm households included a number of kids, oftentimes ten or more. Everyone was poor, but my family was perhaps a little better off than some of our neighbors. Feeding, clothing, and providing shelter for a household of six or more was a formidable task, much more so than providing for a family of three. Nonetheless, ours was a typical rural household in the thirties, and I believe my life as a boy on the farm was representative of the lives of thousands of my peers. We shared the same culture, customs, farm responsibilities, church activities, education opportunities, social life, extended family relationships, and career opportunities.

However, there was one major difference between my life as an only child and that of other farm boys with numerous siblings. I did not have brothers and sisters to play with, so I was forced to entertain myself a good portion of the time. I was blessed with a wild imagination, so I played a lot of make-believe games. You name it, and I probably played it at one time or another. I owned several dolls even though I was a boy, but those dolls were not store-bought. Mother and Grandma Hill made my stuffed dolls from fertilize sacks, embroidery thread, and cotton. You will not believe the number of fights and wars those dolls fought as I grew up. I actually played house (shudder) with dolls when Bonnie, my nearby cousin, came for a visit. My favorite dolls were Whistlebritches and Suzannah, whose names came from Daddy.

I was an avid reader of the Sunday funnies, comic books, the popular Big Little Books, and any other magazines or books I could get my hands on. I knew all the comic book heroes of that era, and I acted out their roles in my mind. I made believe I was

Tarzan, Flash Gordon, the Lone Ranger, Sir Lancelot the Knight, Superman, Gene Autry, Captain Marvel, Buck Rogers, Dick Tracy, Hop-Along Cassidy, and all the other heroes. My vivid imagination carried me on a lot of pulsating adventures; in his mind, a young lad on the farm led an exciting life.

I played ball a lot by myself. I threw a baseball straight up as high as I could and ran to catch it; I threw the ball on top of our house and caught it when it came down; and I bounced a rubber ball off the side of our barn and caught it on the rebound. I got a lot of exercise batting a ball as far as I could and then chasing it down. We did not buy my bat and baseball at a store; they were homemade. I found a sapling tree in the woods, cut it down, and fashioned a bat from a section of that tree. I peeled the bark off the tree section and tapered one end to provide a bat handle. I made my baseball from an abundance of twine string. I found a small round rock and wound the string tightly around the rock until the ball was the desired size. I then sewed the surface of the ball repeatedly with a needle and heavy thread to prevent the twine from unwinding, and presto, I had a new baseball. I do not remember owning a real baseball and bat when I was growing up.

Money was scarce, so most of my toys were homemade. I made excellent whistles from three-inch sections of green hickory branches using a pocket knife. My slingshot, a staple in any young farm boy's arsenal, I made from a forked section of a tree branch, two strips of an old inner tube, and a piece of leather. I used small stones or marbles as "bullets" to kill birds and snakes, and I shot up bottles, tin cans, mail boxes, and any other targets I could find. I was quite good with a slingshot. I received a cap pistol and holster set from Santa one year, but most of my toy guns were homemade. I used a pocket knife to carve pistol shapes from thin flat boards, and those pistols were my weapons of choice in mock battles with cattle rustlers, bank robbers, outlaws, Indians, and other bad guys. A young lad on the farm was one tough hombre in those make-believe confrontations.

I made stilts from two poles, two blocks of wood, and two leather straps. They worked great. One of my favorite pastimes was rolling, or pushing, a small metal hoop around using a stick or narrow board with a U-shaped strip of tin nailed to its end. My horseshoe set consisted of two scrap metal rods and several discarded horseshoes previously used to shod horses. I loved to fly kites, but we never bought one; I made my own. I constructed a kite with brown wrapping paper, two lightweight sticks tied together in the shape of a cross, a bottle of glue, strips of old cloth for a tail, and a roll of twine string, all readily available in farm households. If I did not have glue, I substituted flour mixed with water. My cousins and I sometimes had kite fights. We tied a piece of dried corn stalk or a light stick to the kite's tail to make a weapon. We made the kite dive and pull up sharply a few feet from the ground. The corn stalk tail then slapped anyone standing underneath the kite.

My bow was a three-foot hickory branch bent into the shape of a bow and held in place by a piece of fishing cord or baling wire. My arrows consisted of several pointed sticks, notched on one end, with feathers tied around the notched ends. My homemade bow and arrows were crude but functional. Those are typical examples of playthings produced by energetic and creative country kids with little money; I was one of many thousands of such youngsters in the thirties. The satisfaction realized in "inventing" those toys equaled the enjoyment experienced in using them.

One of my hobbies as a young lad was collecting Indian arrowheads. Native Americans apparently lived in our area at one time because arrowheads showed up in our fields occasionally after a rain. The rain washed the soil away from the arrowheads so they were exposed, and after we plowed the field again, subsequent rains sometimes uncovered additional arrowheads. I walked across our fields at times searching for arrowheads, but I usually found them while plowing or hoeing; I just happened to spot one periodically. I did not have a large collection, but my daughter, Debbie, mounted them in a nice frame. They are now hanging on the wall in my living room.

I kept up with sports as best I could as far back as I remember. We had limited media coverage of sports activities outside our local area, so I was not cognizant of most happenings around the sports world. I did get to see the sports section of our local newspaper occasionally, and we listened to boxing and a little baseball on the radio. For some unknown reason, a rural farm boy in Northeast Texas adopted the Brooklyn Dodgers as his baseball team, and he followed them faithfully. The St. Louis Cardinals were the major league baseball team nearest to Texas, so most sports fans in my neck of the woods supported them, but not me.

I knew Dixie Walker, Pete Reiser, Pee Wee Reese, Eddie Stanky, Carl Furillo, Hugh Casey, Jackie Robinson, and all the other Dodger greats by name, and I kept up with them in their fierce rivalry with the New York Giants. I followed the Dodgers West to Los Angeles and remain a Dodger fan today. A lot of men and boys listened to boxing matches on the radio, with the Joe Louis heavyweight championship fights being the feature attractions. I vaguely recall listening to Joe Louis' match with "Two Ton" Tony Galento in 1939, but I clearly remember his first fight with Billy Conn in 1941. My family attended a social event of some kind that night, probably a pie supper, at the old Methodist Church in Knight's Bluff. A group of men and boys gathered around a battery-powered radio outside the church and listened to the championship match, but all were disappointed when our "great white hope" was knocked out by Joe Louis in the thirteenth round.

One of my earliest memories is an incident involving my small dog Bounce and a half-grown kitten. I was holding the kitten and Bounce began barking at him. The frightened kitten started climbing on me to get away from the dog. I picked up the scared kitten and set him on top of my blonde bare head; that was a huge mistake. You can imagine what that terrified kitten's claws did to my scalp. Needless to say, I never tried that stunt again, and strange as it seems, that is my only recollection of Bounce.

I was an only child, but I did have playmates a good portion of the time. We lived adjacent to two of my cousins, Doyle and Bonnie, and the three of us spent a great deal of time together, either at their house or at mine. We enjoyed a variety of outside games, including baseball, hide-and-seek, tag, jump rope, hop scotch, horseshoes, Annie over, washers, marbles, and others. Various cousins visited at times, especially on Sundays, and we played cowboys and Indians, robbed wasp nests, played ball, went swimming, climbed trees, hunted birds, engaged in corn cob fights, and got involved in all sorts of activities, some approved by our parents and others not.

We were reckless at times so some of the things we did were dangerous, and one of us wound up hurt more than once. I remember a time we were involved in a fierce corn cob fight in Uncle Charlie's barn. Some of us were on the ground and others were in the hay loft, madly hurling corn cobs at one another. One of my cousins in the hay loft, I believe it was Harold, got hit in the head with a corn cob. On another occasion, we were playing outside and someone, probably me, shoved Edgar into a wash pot full of dirty water. His clothes were ruined, so he had to wear one of Bonnie's gowns home. His parents stopped at Watkins Country Store on the way home, and Edgar hid on the floor board of their car so no one would see him.

A group of us were hunting snakes one day along the creek running across our pasture. We killed a large water moccasin, and a neighbor boy decided to show us how to pop off a snake's head. He was swinging the snake around like a whip and it slipped out of his hand, wrapping itself around Harold's neck. I have never seen a more startled look than the one on Harold's face. Think about it; what would your reaction be if a big snake was suddenly draped around your neck?

After dark one night, a few of my cousins and I took Edgar on his first "snipe hunt." Note the ringleader in all those escapades; it was yours truly. We took him into the dark pasture near the creek. Edgar held the sack, and the rest of us left, supposedly to make a big circle and beat the bushes to run the snipe (birds) into the bag. But, we sneaked off and hid quietly behind a clump of bushes. Edgar waited a few minutes and began to call us. No one answered , of course, and he realized he had been duped. We followed behind him at a distance as he made his way back to the house.

Doyle, Edgar, Harold, and I wrestled for hours when we got together on Sundays. Doyle was two years older than me, I was one year older than Edgar, and Edgar was one year older than Harold. Doyle was a big strong boy for his age, whereas Edgar,

Harold, and I were scrawny little guys. The three of us teamed up against Doyle, but we were never able to beat him. He manhandled us any way he pleased. Harold did get the best of Doyle, however, on one occasion. For some reason, I do not recall why, he became very angry with Doyle, grabbed him by the ear, and yanked him to the ground. Doyle yielded to Harold that time.

We celebrated Christmas every year, but Santa's sleigh always carried a light load. I woke up each Christmas morning with a lot of excitement and with great expectations, very much like youngsters today, and I was never disappointed. Santa invariably left me one big toy plus candy, nuts, fruit, and two or three small items. My main toy was a little red wagon one year, a pistol and holster set on another, a tricycle on yet another Christmas, a set of Chinese checkers one year, or some similar plaything each year. I was thrilled with those great Santa gifts, and I played with each one of them for years. Kids back then did not have much, so we did not get bored with our toys and cast them aside.

Farm folks in the thirties and forties did not celebrate Christmas to the same extent people do today; they could not afford it. A lot of families put up Christmas trees, but they decorated them with homemade ornaments. Occasionally, we did buy icicles for the tree, but not much else. I remember going into the woods before Christmas and cutting down a small cedar or pine tree. We constructed a stand for it and designed our own ornaments. Painted sweet gum balls and pine cones made great ornaments, and we made ropes from small strips of paper glued in circles and looped together. We also decorated the tree with sprigs of mistletoe and holly berries. We utilized virtually any colorful thing we found in the woods as ornaments. None of the people I knew had inside or outside decorations other than Christmas trees. We had no electricity, hence we had no lights.

Children today have an insatiable appetite, and we were no different. Kids demanded their regular snacks, especially after school. But, none of our snacks were bought; they were home grown or homemade. Mother baked a lot of cookies and muffins, and she fried dried apple and dried peach pies. Other favorite snacks of mine included baked sweet potatoes, a biscuit and onion, a biscuit with jelly, a large tomato from our garden, parched peanuts, sausage and biscuit, and fresh fruit from our orchard. Mothers, when your precious little one comes home from school starving, give him or her a biscuit and onion and see how he or she reacts.

I enjoyed my after-school snack every day, and I was also assigned my after-school chores. I helped with the field work during the farming season if I got home from school early enough. I was assigned household chores instead on those days I got home too late to go to the fields. I gathered eggs and put out feed for the chickens and pigs. I often shucked and shelled corn using a hand-cranked corn sheller, and I sometimes drove in the livestock if they did not come to the barn on their own. I did those chores as far back as I can recall. I can't remember not having any work to do while I was growing up; work was simply part of life on the farm.

Farming was a seasonal occupation, so kids did have a lot of idle time throughout the year. We never did field work on Sundays, so we had a lot of free time then. I started hunting birds with Daddy's 22 rifle or my slingshot at a very young age; I do not remember learning to shoot a rifle. I killed few birds with my slingshot, but I was a good marksman with the 22 rifle. I found it a real challenge to line up two birds at one time and kill both of them with one shot. I fed the many birds I killed to our cats, and they usually met me as I neared the house after a bird hunting foray. The cats were excited and climbed on me trying to get to the dead birds. I also constructed bird traps and caught a small number of birds, including cardinals, but I never tried to keep them in a cage like some folks did. I just turned my captured prey loose.

I hunted squirrels occasionally with Uncle Charlie or some of my cousins, but there were few squirrels in the woods near us, and we did not have a squirrel dog. We were lucky to bag one squirrel in a half day of hunting. That was not the case, however, for folks who lived near the vast Suphur River bottom land. It was not unusual for a hunter to kill several dozen squirrels in one outing on Sulphur River. Quail hunting was a popular sport for a lot of men and boys, but hunting quail required a bird dog and a shotgun, and all I had was a

22 rifle. I did go quail hunting with Kenneth and Wayne a couple of times, but I never tried to shoot the birds.

Fishing was a very popular sport when I was growing up, especially along the winding Sulphur River. A nice spring-fed creek ran through our pasture, providing year-round water for livestock, an ample supply of small perch for a young fisherman, and a breeding place for poisonous water moccasins. I spent many hours digging worms and catching grasshoppers for bait and fishing along that creek. I caught a lot of small catfish and perch, but seldom took them home to eat; I threw my catch back into the creek most of the time. I walked two miles to the Sulphur River a few times for a day of fishing. I walked the two miles to the river in the morning, fished up and down the river bank several hours, and walked back home. Those were fruitless fishing excursions for the most part.

I was afraid of snakes when I lived on the farm, and my fear of them has not diminished to this day. I was always watchful for snakes when fishing or swimming in our creek, and I watched closely for snakes each time I crossed the creek on the way to and from our fields. I was on the way home from the field one day and started to crawl under a barbed wire fence a few feet from the creek. Just as I got my head under the fence, I glanced forward into the face of a huge coiled water moccasin ready to strike. That was some shock for me, and my head probably snapped back like a turtle's head going back into its shell.

The creek crossing our pasture originated in Uncle Charlie's pasture adjacent to ours, and it meandered through several farms downstream from us. The creek was wide enough and deep enough in one place in our pasture to accommodate limited swimming, provided the snakes were scared off and the surface scum was splashed away. My cousins and I dammed up the creek on numerous occasions to provide a larger swimming hole, but subsequent rains always washed the dams away. We skinny-dipped in our small temporary swimming hole or walked to Mr. Upchurch's adjacent farm and went skinny-dipping in his larger stock pond. We also swam in the Sulphur River during the times we were there for family picnics or fishing trips. Some of my older cousins and their friends used a horse-drawn slip to build a large dam across the creek in Uncle Charlie's pasture, providing a large swimming pond. That is where Doyle learned to swim. His older brother, Clyde, threw him into the pond and told him to sink or swim, and he swam.

A majority of my peers did not wear shoes, even to school. Virtually all boys and a lot of girls went barefooted during warm weather. My work uniform in the fields was overalls or jeans and a wide-brimmed straw hat (no shoes, no shirt, no belt, and no underwear). Going barefooted did lead to three significant problems, however. Stubbing one's toe, which happened frequently doing farm work, was quite painful, sometimes causing the loss of a toenail. Walking in an area infested with grass burrs (stickers) was also painful. I found it frustrating to walk to the middle of a grassy area without incident, step on a grass burr, and stop to remove it, only to discover that any direction I walked was loaded with stickers. Experience told me the best thing to do was grit my teeth, walk briskly out of the infested area without stopping, and then stop and remove the stickers from my feet. Hot sand was another nemesis for bare feet. Walking slow through deep sand burned one's bare feet like crazy when the sun was hot. I found it less painful to run through hot sand rather than walk.

Queen City or Atlanta was the nearest place for us to shop, and both were some ten miles away, but we did not own a car until I was in high school. Our school bus driver made a run to Queen City and Atlanta each Saturday, picking up folks to do their weekly shopping. I often stayed home on Saturday to help Daddy with the crops, so Mother caught the bus by herself to buy staple groceries we needed, feed for chickens and livestock, household goods, and clothes we were in need of. Mother made most of our clothes or ordered them from the Sears & Roebuck mail-order catalog. She also ordered a lot of household goods from Sears & Roebuck. I went to town with Mother on Saturdays when we were caught up with the field work, and Daddy joined us sometimes in the off seasons.

Saturday shopping was an all-day affair. The bus driver made stops at Gilley's General Store and John D. Hanes Store in Queen City, and he parked the bus several hours in downtown

Atlanta. We bought a majority of our goods at Gilley's, an old but huge retail establishment which stocked everything a farm family needed. Mr. and Mrs. Gilley sold farm implements, hardware, livestock and chicken feed, fertilizers, clothing, groceries, sporting goods, and all kinds of household items. The old Gilley's building remains today. It is closed, but I suspect you could find some stock left over from the thirties and forties if you went inside. Gilley's Store is truly a historic reminder of the early 1900s in Cass County.

Atlanta was home to a number of drugstores, clothing stores, hardware stores, variety stores, grocery stores, and other retailers, so our bus folks did a lot of their shopping there. The most important business for me in Atlanta was the movie theater, or picture show. Saturday was cowboy show day, and I went to see my heroes perform as often as my parents would allow. I saw the entire show most Saturdays, but Mother or Daddy came into the theater and called me out sometimes if the bus was due to leave soon. The highlight of my Saturday shopping trip was that cowboy picture show, but I also looked forward to getting a Dixie Cup (ice cream cup) with a movie star's picture inside the lid. I saved those lids and accumulated a good selection of movie star pictures. A Baby Ruth or Butterfinger candy bar was also a real treat on those Saturday trips to town.

I was a country music fan as far back as I remember. I listened faithfully to the Grand Ole Opry from Nashville, Tennessee, every Saturday night on our battery-powered radio. Minnie Pearl, Eddy Arnold, Ernest Tubb, Roy Acuff, Uncle Dave Macon, and Red Foley were a few of my favorite Opry stars. I recently stood on the stage of the historic Ryman Auditorium where hundreds of country music stars performed since 1943. That was an awesome experience. KWKH radio in Shreveport, Louisiana, broadcast a lot of country music in the thirties and forties, and I was one of their regular listeners. My favorite singer was Ernest Tubb, the Texas Troubadour, and I gave my rendition of his first big hit, "Walking the Floor Over You," many times while walking behind a plow or chopping cotton. My cousins and I argued constantly about who was the best country singer. I maintained Ernest Tubb was the best, but some of them chose Eddy Arnold.

I had three faithful dogs as companions while growing up. I barely remember the first one, Bounce. Daddy Brown gave me the second one, Bugs, and he spent quite a few years in our household. We romped and played many hours, so much so that it interfered with my assigned chores at times. I obtained my third dog, Rip, when he was a tiny puppy, and he was my constant companion until I finished high school and moved away from home. Rip went to the fields with me, he was my bird hunting buddy, he was my fishing partner, and he was a part of our rat-killing team.

Very few farm kids owned bicycles in the thirties and forties. Edgar was the first one in our extended family to get a bicycle, and I believe it was a 26-inch girl's model because he was too small to safely handle a large boy's bike with a top bar. I learned to ride on his bike, and I got my first bicycle shortly afterward. I sold a calf Daddy had given me and used the money to buy a used bicycle. If I remember correctly, I paid fifteen dollars for it. My bike was a 24-inch boy's single-speed model, which I could handle safely. I rode my bike to school at Knight's Bluff, a one and one-half mile ride on dirt roads. I navigated most of that distance with few problems, but one section of the road contained deep sandy ruts. I was unable to pedal my single-speed bike through the deep sand, so I walked the bike a short distance each trip. I rode my bike to school, rain or shine, and I rode it up and down the roads around our house. I enjoyed my "wheels."

Daddy bought our first car when I was in high school, a used Ford Model T coupe, for which he paid sixty-five dollars. Thank goodness, we did not have to ride the school bus to town for shopping after that. Mother learned to drive, and she and I took off to Queen City and Atlanta almost every Saturday to do our weekly shopping. We also drove the car to church rather than walk, and we did not have to walk when we visited Mama Brown and Daddy Brown. We cranked our Model T by hand to start it, and that old jalopy required a lot of cranking at times, especially in cold weather. Mother and I often wore ourselves out trying to get our car started.

1925 Ford Model T

That Model T had insufficient power to climb some of the steep hills on the dirt roads we traveled. I got out of the car a few times and pushed to help it climb steep hills. On one occasion, I was supposed to steer while Mother pushed, and I steered our Model T into a deep ditch; I was not the best driver in the world at that time. A farmer who lived nearby pulled us out of the ditch and up the hill with his tractor. Mother ran into a tree in Aunt Mildred's front yard on another one of our escapades; she was not a great driver either. We experienced some wild times in that old jalopy, but it was better than walking. I learned to drive our Model T although I was too young to get a driver's license.

My bedroom in the last house I lived in on the farm was next to the front porch, so when nature called at night or early in the morning, I simply stepped out on the porch to take care of business. That practice led to embarrassing moments at times. Occasionally, a car topped the hill near our house and caught me before I was finished, an awkward incident. Two teenage sisters lived about one-half mile down a side road in front of us, and they waited for the school bus at our house each morning. And guess what. They walked into our yard one morning while I was taking care of business on the front porch. I looked up and saw them a few feet away and quickly darted back into the house. They did not say anything, and neither did I, but I am sure they had a good laugh afterward.

I was caught in a similar situation while plowing in our back field one day. An old road bed ran through our farm, and people sometimes walked that old road as a shortcut between Antioch and Blalock communities. I was plowing in our field adjacent to the old road bed and had an urge to use the bathroom. I stopped my horse at the end of the row and walked across the road about fifteen feet and found a suitable spot. I squatted comfortably and was minding my own business when I heard voices. Two ladies walked by between me and my horse, just a few feet from where I was squatting. They did not speak and neither did I; they just passed by looking straight ahead. I finished and resumed my plowing, somewhat embarrassed.

A large number of farm kids were uninterested in school and thus did not enjoy reading. But, not me. I was an avid bookworm as far back as I remember. I read comic books, the Sunday funnies, a newspaper when I had the chance, Big Little Books, school library books, Life magazines, western novels, Bonnie's True Romance magazines, or any other reading material I got my hands on. I had no one to play with a good portion of the time, I had a lot of idle time during the farming off-season, and I possessed an inquisitive mind, so reading was an enjoyable and rewarding pastime for me. Reading opened up a world I was not exposed to on the farm, and my intense desire and advanced ability to read helped me tremendously as I pursued a high school education, and ultimately, an engineering degree.

Farming was the only life I knew growing up, but I subconsciously yearned for something more. I was a happy youngster, I enjoyed farm work, I lived a good life, and I harbored no grand aspirations beyond high school, but I was not content to remain on the farm after graduation. I graduated from Atlanta High School in 1947 at age fourteen, moved to Atlanta a few months later, and relocated to Shreveport, Louisiana, at sixteen years of age, thus ending my life on the farm. That was my first time to be as far as sixty miles away from my birth place.

6.
One-Room One-Teacher School

E lementary schools in the thirties were not consolidated. Each community claimed its own grade school, and country kids rode school buses to Queen City and Atlanta for consolidated high school classes. Students in our community attended Knight's Bluff School through the eighth grade, rode a school bus ten to twelve miles to Queen City for grades nine and ten, and rode the bus a few more miles to Atlanta for grades eleven and twelve. The Knight's Bluff School closed at the end of the 1947 school year, and students from all grades rode the school bus to Queen City in subsequent years.

Most rural communities in that region of Cass County featured two-room two-teacher elementary schools, but communities with fewer residents got by with one-room one-teacher schools. Knight's Bluff community claimed one of the smaller schools, whereas adjacent Antioch and Blalock communities featured larger two-room schoolhouses. The ratio of students to teachers was fifteen to twenty back then, so Knight's Bluff School served fifteen to twenty students spread across eight grades, one grade per row or half-row of desks. A grade sometimes consisted of four or five students, but other grades contained only one or two kids each. All students were present in that one room when a class was in session; you could either listen to the class in session or do homework.

I am not certain, but I believe the teachers in those rural schools received salaries based on the number of students they taught. One child thus had an appreciable impact on a teacher's salary. A child had to be six years old on September 1 in order to qualify for school that year, and I missed the deadline by seven days in 1938. Mrs. Carroll, the teacher, told Daddy to send me to school anyway, although she was not paid for teaching me that first year. I missed the first week of my initial year in school, but I quickly caught up with the other kids.

Bonnie, Doyle, and I lived next door to one another, but we were in different school districts. I was in the Knight's Bluff district, and they were in the Antioch district. For some reason, however, Doyle and Bonnie attended Knight's Bluff School with me for two or three years, and we walked to school together. After that, Doyle and Bonnie walked to Antioch School and I continued in Knight's Bluff. I walked alone, or with some neighbor boys occasionally, until I got my bicycle, and then I rode it to school.

We could either walk the dirt road to Knight's Bluff School or take a shortcut through some woods. We chose the shortcut, a distance of approximately one mile. We walked a relatively smooth trail through a wooded area by an old sawmill site, down a steep hill and across the Boiler Branch, up another hill to the dirt road, and on to school. We walked to school, rain or shine, and we never stayed home because of inclement weather. We froze when it was cold and got soaked when it rained, but occasionally a neighbor passing us in a car gave us a ride to school or home. I remember sitting down and scooting on my rear end up or down that steep hill when snow or ice was on the ground; I could not stand up on the icy ground.

We often stopped on the way home from school and played on a huge pile of sawdust at the old sawmill site, so we were sometimes late getting home. Mother and Daddy were not happy with me being late, because I had chores to do. We went to school barefooted in warm weather, but our parents insisted that we wear shoes when the weather turned nippy. Our shoes did not always get to school, however. We pulled them off in the morning and hid them at the old sawmill site and picked them up on the way home in the afternoon. Doyle, Bonnie, and I were not alone in disobeying our parents regarding shoes. Doyle's older brother, Clyde, and his older sister, Vaudine, set a precedent for us when they walked to Antioch School a few years earlier. They hid their shoes in bushes in the morning and retrieved them in the afternoon on the way home. Vaudine said she could not tell their parents because Clyde threatened to whip her if she did, and he was five years older than her. I am sure a lot of other kids left home wearing shoes but arrived at school barefooted. Shoes cramped our style back then; shoes were not cool.

I had only one pair of school shoes, the same as every other kid. The gals wore shoes more than the guys, but some girls went barefooted as often as their parents would allow. A quick fix for a shoe with a hole worn through the sole was a piece of cardboard inserted inside the shoe; you made do with what you had. Occasionally, a girl would wear a shoe with the front half of her shoe sole pulled away from the shoe, so the sole would flop up and down as she walked. The girl remedied that problem by picking up her foot to allow the loose sole to flop in place before she put her foot down. Her stride was not too graceful, but again, you played the hand you were dealt.

Most kids had two sets of school clothes; you wore one set a week and wore the other set the next week. Holes in clothes were patched, so it was not unusual to see a kid with several patches on his pants, especially the knees. We were not style conscience. A few unfortunate folks were unable to buy adequate clothing for their children, so they depended on hand-me-down apparel from their extended family or neighbors. I know that some of my outgrown clothes were passed on to cousins or neighbor kids. Those secondhand clothes were often the wrong size or patched all over, but needy kids were happy to get them. We did not criticize or make fun of other kids' clothing because all of us were in the same boat. I suspect all of us looked like little ragamuffins.

I walked to school before I bought my bicycle, but I rode my bike the one and one-half miles to Knight's Bluff School after that. I was not allowed to ride my bike at school, so I parked it in the Old Methodist Church building when school was in session. No one was concerned about theft in those days. I was the only kid in school with a bicycle, so the other kids often asked if they could ride it. I visited my cousins, Kenneth and Wayne, occasionally before I went home, and I permitted some of the kids to ride my bike then. Admittedly, I was selfish with my bicycle, but I paid for it with my own money, and I did not want it torn up.

The Knight's Bluff schoolhouse consisted of one large classroom, a small front porch, and a cloak room adjacent to the porch. A long blackboard hung on the back wall behind the teacher's desk, and a row of side-by-side windows covered one entire side wall. The walls and ceiling utilized plain painted lumber, and the floor was wood as well. The classroom was heated by a huge wood-burning pot-bellied heater in a front corner next to the cloak room. Wood for the heater was stored in a wooden box behind the heater. The schoolhouse did not have electricity, so light for schoolwork was provided by the row of windows. Several rows of small desks faced the teacher's desk, and each student was assigned a desk. Pencils, pens, paper, ink, books, and other personal supplies were stored in the students' desks. Coats, library books, and other school supplies were stored in the cloak room.

The schoolhouse was encircled by a large dirt playground, with the front section large enough to accommodate a small softball field. Long fly balls often carried into the bushes outside the playground, so outfielders had to exercise caution when chasing a fly ball. The schoolhouse and playground were located a few hundred feet from the dirt road, directly behind an old Methodist Church. Regular church services were no longer conducted in the church building, but community social events, pie suppers, special religious services, and other such activities utilized the building occasionally.

Neighbors met prior to the start of school each year to clear weeds and grass from the school playground. We had dirt yards at home and a dirt playground at school. An old log arbor with a roof and low log walls sat on one corner of the playground near the church building. I never knew why the log arbor was built originally, perhaps for use in church revivals, but it provided a nice covered area for community-wide pot stews and a fun playhouse for the school kids. We spent a lot of time climbing on that old arbor.

Drinking water for the school was supplied by a well at one edge of the school playground. As I recall, a manual pump was installed atop the covered well, and water was pumped by hand into an elevated water barrel. A pipe from the barrel enabled students to drink water from it. A manual pump such as the one used in the Knight's Bluff School lost its prime at times. When that occurred, the teacher sent two of the older boys to fetch a bucket of water from a spring below the playground to prime the pump. The spring was down a steep hill a little ways from the well, so carrying water up the hill to prime the pump was quite a chore.

Students in the eight grades were lined up in order in the classroom, with the eighth grade occupying the row of desks closest to the windows and the first grade assigned to the row of desks across the classroom from the windows. But, the kids were not always lined up by age. Some families kept their kids home in the fall until the crops were harvested, and then pulled them out of school early in the spring to help plant crops for the next year. As a result, those part-time students were seldom promoted to the next grade, so they remained in the same grade two or three years. The lower grades were thus made up of youngsters six to eight years of age, together with much larger kids, usually boys, ten to thirteen years old.

It was a strange sight to see small eight year old kids in the same class with large thirteen year old boys. But listening to those older boys struggle with second and third grade class work, especially reading, was even stranger. That experience was somewhat comical to the rest of us at the time, but it was a sad commentary on the priorities set by some parents on an education for their children. Times were hard, most families depended on help from their kids on the farm, and a lot of parents did not appreciate the value of an education for their kids. I was one of the fortunate few. My parents encouraged me to get a high school education and thus seldom kept me out of school to help with the farm work. I can count on my fingers the total number of days my parents kept me out of school to help plant or harvest the crops.

Rural schools in the thirties did not have electricity or running water, so we did not have inside bathrooms. We relied on outhouses instead. The wood frame guy's facility was located in the woods a short distance from one side of the playground, and a similar toilet for the gals was situated in the woods on the opposite side of the schoolhouse. The federal government supplied various commodities to schools for distribution to the families of school children. Knight's Bluff School received several crates of eggs on one such occasion. Everyone raised chickens at home, so none of the students took the eggs. The eggs spoiled, and the teacher sent three or four boys to dump the eggs in the woods. We "dumped" the eggs as instructed, but we dumped them by throwing them at the girl's outhouse. I do not recall if we were punished for that deed or not.

Kids brought lunches to school, except for those students who lived nearby; they walked home for lunch. Helen, Kenneth, and Wayne lived near the school so they walked home for lunch. Our typical lunch fare was homemade biscuits with melted butter and sugar, sausage biscuits, biscuits with preserves or jelly, peanut butter and crackers, fresh fruit from the orchard, tomatoes from the garden, homemade cookies or fried fruit pies, or baked sweet potatoes. Baked sweet potatoes were probably our favorites; they were tasty and filling, and everyone grew potatoes at home. A big soft sweet potato made quite a mess when one of the boys, yours truly excluded, threw it on the side of the schoolhouse. I do not remember who cleaned those big blobs of sweet potatoes off the schoolhouse.

You are probably thinking, "What kind of education did those country bumpkins get under such primitive conditions?" Well, we received a quality education strong in the basics. Both Mrs. Carroll, my first teacher, and Mrs. Wilson, my second teacher, gave us a good dose of reading, writing, and arithmetic, the three R's. In addition, we studied literature, grammar, geography, history, health, civics, and music. Students from rural schools experienced minimal difficulties in competing with city kids in high school classes at Queen City and Atlanta. The few rural high school students who had problems were those kept out of school by their parents to help with the farm work. It is also doubtful that they received encouragement at home regarding school work.

To some extent, youngsters in small one-teacher and two-teacher schools enjoyed advantages over students in larger schools. Teachers in small schools devoted more one-on-one attention to each student, so the students advanced academically at a rate commensurate with their inherent abilities. Schools did not offer honors classes back then, but teachers pushed students to perform at high levels, and teachers at small rural schools were able to provide greater assistance to children who excelled in school work. Several students at Knight's Bluff School were promoted two grades in one year, including yours truly. I completed eight grades in five years at Knight's Bluff School, so I graduated from high school at age fourteen. I did not skip any grade school course work, however; I completed all the required classes in each of the eight grades.

I remember taking classes in two grades at the same time; I received two report cards each six weeks, one for each grade. I could not have accomplished that feat without the encouragement and extra help I received from the teachers. I was three or four years younger than my classmates in high school at Queen City and Atlanta, yet I experienced few academic problems. I lagged behind my classmates socially, but that did not present a problem academically; I simply socialized with kids in lower grades. Other students I knew who were promoted at an accelerated rate in rural schools also managed to compete with older students at the high school level. And, I was not at a disadvantage in studying for my Electrical Engineering degree in college. So, I do not consider those small rural elementary schools to be inferior to the larger city schools of that time period.

Unlike today, elementary schools in the thirties required minimal special equipment. Calculators, computers, copiers, and other high-tech gadgets represented education tools of the future and were thus not required. School work was performed manually, so students learned to read and write, skills not mastered by many of today's students. Kids in small rural schools also engaged in a lot of group classroom activities which encouraged participation by everyone and created competition among classmates. Teachers led us in spelling bees, math drills, group singing, group discussions, and other group functions, all fun activities which motivated us to excel and enhanced our learning abilities.

A lady, perhaps the school district superintendent, visited our school periodically to check with the teacher and deliver library books, playground equipment, and other school supplies. She also picked up old library books as she dropped off the new ones. I was an avid reader, so I looked forward to getting a new batch of books to read. I faithfully checked out and read each library book before she brought a new set. The lady also brought us a new softball, a bat, or some other playground item occasionally. I remember one time when she brought a new catcher's mitt for one of the boys. I am not sure why she gave it to Gene, but he must have won it as some kind of prize. In any event, that was the only baseball glove in Knight's Bluff School at the time. We caught a batted ball or a thrown ball with bare hands, and catching a new ball before it was broken in (roughed up and softened) really smarted. We did not play football or basketball at Knight's Bluff School.

A good portion of our classroom work involved group activities, and our playground time was no different. Most of the games during recess and lunch times included all the kids. Softball was our favorite game, but we participated in all kinds of running and jumping activities. We ran races, played tag, popped the whip with a long line of kids, played Annie over, and played dodge ball, among others. School children in the thirties and forties were not obese like a lot of children today. A diet heavy in fruits and vegetables, plenty of exercise, and hard work kept the pounds off. We did not spend hours each day in front of television, surfing on a computer, playing video games, texting our friends, and listening to the latest fad music. Neither did we eat our meals in fast food restaurants, drink a lot of soft drinks, nor order take-out pizza. We ate healthy and exercised regularly, and it showed.

Our teacher took us on field trips occasionally. A group of larger kids visited Antioch School one time for a softball game; I do not recall who won, but most likely it was not us. The entire school trekked through the woods for a few hours fishing along a creek on another occasion. I do not remember us catching any fish, but I did snag a nice one which fell off the hook before I could get it to the bank; the big one always gets away. Do you remember those older boys in the lower grades who struggled with their reading? Well, they were the stars in our softball games and other competitive activities.

There were a lot of chores to do around school, but we did not have a janitorial service. The flag on the flagpole was raised and lowered each day, the blackboard and erasers required regular cleaning, water was fetched when needed to prime the well pump, firewood for the pot-bellied heater was needed each day in cold weather, rotten eggs and other spoiled commodities had to be dumped, water was pumped into the water barrel each day, and various other chores filled the agenda. The teacher assigned chores to various students, so we had jobs to do at school as well as jobs to do at home.

Students often disobeyed the teacher, violated school rules, or acted up in class. Our misdeeds included talking while a class was in session, shooting spit balls, passing notes in class, fighting on the playground, being late for school, hanging around the playground after school was out, and other similar violations. Our punishment varied, depending on the severity of the infraction. An unruly student, usually a boy, sometimes sat on a chair in the corner facing the wall, or he stood facing the blackboard with his nose in a ring drawn on the blackboard. Another favorite punishment meted out by the teacher required the guilty party to write, "I will not talk in class" or "I will not pass notes in school" one hundred times.

The old standby, of course, was the paddle, which was reserved for more serious offences. And, I do not remember a parent complaining to the teacher about her paddling their child. In fact, if a student received a paddling in school, he or she most likely received a more severe whipping at home. I remember one "group" paddling in particular. Students were prohibited from hanging around the playground after school was out, a rule strictly enforced. A group of boys decided to play softball after school let out one day. The game was going great until the teacher returned to school; we never knew why she came back. Mrs. Carroll lined us up on the school porch and dusted our britches with her paddle. For a small lady, she wielded a mean paddle.

The old Knight's Bluff School building is still standing today, as shown on the cover of this book. The school building is not visible from the paved road in front of it; the old Methodist Church and log arbor are long gone; the two outhouses are history; and the playground is grown up in trees and underbrush. The school building was converted into a residence after the school was closed. A partition divided the classroom into two rooms, and a kitchen was added on one side, but the exterior remains the same as it was seventy years ago. I went inside that old schoolhouse recently, and it was an awesome experience to stand in the one-room schoolhouse where I attended classes from 1938 until 1943.

7.

City School

S tudents in Queen City, Atlanta, and surrounding rural communities attended high school in Queen City and/or Atlanta. Queen City High School offered only grades nine and ten in the thirties and early forties, so all students in the entire area attended Atlanta High School for grades eleven and twelve. Students from rural elementary schools in the Queen City school district rode buses to Queen City for grades nine and ten and transferred to Atlanta for their junior and senior years. Included in those rural communities in the Queen City district were Antioch, Knight's Bluff, Blalock, and Courtland, all on the same school bus route. Other bus routes served students living in neighboring communities in the Queen City district.

I do not know who owned the school buses in that time period, either the school districts or the drivers, but the bus drivers kept the buses at their homes and used them for non-school purposes. Folks on our route rode the bus to Queen City and Atlanta for Saturday shopping, to Atlanta for Saturday night movies, and to Queen City and Atlanta for other activities. Our bus driver resided in Antioch community, some ten to twelve miles from Queen City, and his meandering route included the Antioch, Knight's Bluff, Blalock, and Courtland communities.

Our bus driver picked up school kids in Antioch community first, picked up the Knight's Bluff students next, made a loop through the Blalock community to pick up students there, picked up the Courtland community kids last, and drove the bus load of students to the Queen City School. The entire route was on the order of fifteen miles, and the driver picked up students at multiple stops all along the way. Some of the kids lived directly on the bus route and thus waited for the bus in their homes, whereas others walked up to one-half mile to catch the bus. They stood in the rain or snow in inclement weather and waited for the bus. I saw boys with wet and frozen hair at times.

After dropping off his load of students at Queen City, our driver made a second run through another community near Queen City to pick up additional kids. Then, he transported the juniors and seniors from both routes to Atlanta High School, another two-mile jaunt. Note that all students were at the Queen City and Atlanta schools prior to the scheduled start of classes, so quite a few of the kids experienced significant wait times in addition to the long rides. That wait time included the time required for the driver to run his second route. The bus driver reversed his path in the afternoon after school was out. He hauled the juniors and seniors from Atlanta to Queen City, ran his short route near Queen City, and then picked up Queen City students for his long route home. He dropped students off in Courtland, Blalock, Knight's Bluff, and Antioch communities as he made his way back home. The afternoon bus route was the identical reverse of the morning route, and it was just as time consuming.

School days for a lot of country kids were extremely long. Students who lived in Antioch and Knight's Bluff communities left home before daylight in the winter time and arrived home from school after sundown. School bus transportation from Antioch and Knight's Bluff to Queen City was not even available prior to the mid-thirties. One of my older cousins, Clyde, wanted to finish high school in Atlanta, but he did not have a way to get to school. He rode a horse ten miles to Atlanta when he started high school. His Uncle Edgar, who lived in Queen City, invited Clyde to live with his family until he finished high school. Clyde did so and rode with his cousin who drove to school every day. That was during the Great Depression, and Clyde's parents did not have any money to pay his Uncle Edgar. But, they shared produce from their garden with him; that was the only payment they could make. Extended families helped one another during those difficult years.

Queen City School was a relatively small city school, comparable to hundreds of other small-town schools in Texas at the time. It contained an elementary school building, a high school building, a small home economics building, and a gymnasium. Indoor bathroom facilities were available, but most of the older boys utilized an outhouse on the edge of the school ground. The boys smoked there and engaged in all kinds of mischief. A large softball field and the gymnasium provided venues for sports activities. Queen City competed with nearby schools in basketball, but did not field teams in baseball, football, or track.

We played softball a lot in school, but basketball was the predominant sport at Queen City. Boys played basketball in the morning while waiting for classes to start, during recess and lunch breaks, and after school while waiting for our bus driver to complete his short route. I am sure we were a bunch of sweaty smelly boys when we piled into the bus for the long ride home. Kids did not bathe daily when I was growing up, houses and schools were not air-conditioned, we wore school clothes several days between washings, we played hard, and deodorant was unheard of, so I am certain we smelled pretty ripe. I do not recall that being a problem for kids from the farm, but the "cleaner" city students and the teachers probably stayed upwind from us.

Each grade in Queen City School consisted of fifteen to twenty students, and each grade had its own homeroom and homeroom teacher. We had different teachers for English, math, history, science, and the other subjects, quite a switch from the one-room one-teacher school I attended in Knight's Bluff. Students did all their school work, including math, by hand; we did not have slide rules, calculators, or any other special tools. Math courses included algebra, trigonometry, and plane geometry, and the only aids we used were math tables.

Expensive educational equipment, other than band instruments, sports equipment, typewriters, and shop equipment, was not required in the thirties and forties. Consequently, our learning experience in the small Queen City School was comparable to that in much larger school districts. The primary advantages enjoyed by large schools over small schools were in the areas of sports, music, typing, and shop. Larger schools offered a variety of sports programs and opportunities to participate in high school bands. Larger schools also offered typing and shop (woodwork) classes.

Country kids blended in well with city youngsters with a few minor exceptions. Rural kids did not have a lot of money to spend like some of their peers who lived in town, so we were unable to buy cokes, ice cream, candy, and other treats, a fact we were well aware of. An appreciable number of rural students went barefooted to school, more so than our classmates living in town, but that was an insignificant issue. Country kids' clothing was probably not up to par with that of city dwellers, but no one seemed to notice; kids back then were not as style conscience as the youth of today.

Probably the greatest difference between rural students and those from the city was our social life. Country youth worked long hours on the farm and therefore did not have a lot of free time for social activities. Also, we lived a relatively long distance apart and did not have transportation, so we were somewhat limited socially. But most important of all, rural kids did not have the financial wherewithal to support an active social agenda. Those differences carried over into high school. Students from rural communities were not as involved in school social functions as were their peers from town. Socially, we were indeed country bumpkins.

Basketball and softball were our primary sports activities at Queen City School, but we participated in other recreational endeavors as well. A few of the boys were avid marble shooters, and we spent many hours at school shooting marbles for "keeps." I was an accomplished marble shooter, compared to some of the other boys, so I won tons of marbles in those games of keeps. I took four or five marbles to school each day and often came home with a pocket full of marbles. That was in addition to the winnings I sometimes sold to the losers for a nickel or a dime; that is how I made money for an occasional ice cream cone, coke, or candy bar. I graduated from high school with a gallon bucket full of marbles, excluding those I shot in my sling shot at birds.

One thing did carry over from Knight's Bluff School to Queen City School, the practice of paddling as a form of punishment for misdeeds. Mr. Hileman, the school superintendent, did all the paddling at Queen City School. Teachers sent misbehaving students to his office and he meted out the punishment, sometimes a verbal reprimand and at other times a paddling. Mr. Hileman made the guilty party bend over with his hands on his knees and then wielded the paddle. I was never the recipient of one of Mr. Hileman's behavior modification sessions, but some of the boys with experience said he was good at his job. I do remember a time when Mr. Hileman gave everyone in one of the classes he taught a failing grade on a test. We were taking a test when the class misbehaved in some manner; I do not recall what we did, but it must have been bad. Whatever the reason, he gave everyone in the class a very low grade on the test, jeopardizing some of the students who had marginally passing grades in the course.

The most notable thing about my high school experience was the long bus ride to and from school. The roads were unpaved; the bus did not have air conditioning; the roads were narrow with deep ditches and a lot of steep hills; passing cars brought clouds of dust into the bus' open windows; and a number of students had to stand up for a portion of the route. Kids living near the start of the route rode the bus well over an hour each way going to school and returning home. Inclement weather led to a lot of problems and increased the time of travel substantially. Older boys piled out of the bus at times to help push the bus up slick and muddy hills, and sleet or snow made driving treacherous. The bus route crossed a low-lying bayou which flooded with every heavy rain. The bus driver often waded through several inches of water to verify the bridge over the bayou was intact before he drove the bus across it. But even with all those problems, I do not recall a time when we failed to get to school in the morning or make it home in the evening.

John D. Hanes Store in Queen City was a gathering place for bus students in the morning and afternoon. The bus driver dropped Atlanta bound juniors and seniors off at Hanes Store before he made his second Queen City route. At the completion of that run, the driver picked up those students and transported them to Atlanta, so the juniors and seniors had about a 45-minute wait. In the afternoon, those same juniors and seniors, along with some of the Queen City students on our route, waited at Hanes Store while the driver made his short Queen City route. Quite a few of the waiting students had money to spend, so they loaded up on candy, soft drinks, cookies, and ice cream cones. Country kids with no money envied those students who had money to spend on treats.

The Atlanta School was appreciably larger than the Queen City School; for example, my graduating class consisted of seventy students, about four times the size of a typical Queen City class. All grades attended school on the same campus, but the elementary school building was across the campus from the high school building, and the playground was somewhat segregated by age group. A small band building and a large gymnasium were near the high school, and a small cafeteria (the Briar Patch) provided lunch for most of the teachers and a lot of students. Atlanta sports teams were called Rabbits, so the cafeteria was named appropriately. My parents gave me twenty-five cents per day to buy lunch. I purchased a hamburger, soft drink, and candy bar for the twenty-five cents, or I bought a hot dog, soft drink, and candy bar for twenty cents, with five cents left to spend at Hanes Store in the afternoon. I was a big spender during my junior and senior years of high school.

Atlanta High School in 1947

82

Academic work in Atlanta High School was comparable to that in Queen City School, but there were a few notable differences. Atlanta offered a broader range of subjects, including typing, shorthand, Spanish, biology, band, and shop, among others. Each class in Atlanta contained a greater number of students, and a huge study hall served all four high school grades. All students utilized the study hall to do homework during their free periods. The study hall included an enclosed library staffed by one of the students. I did a majority of my homework and preparation for classes during study hall time and checked out library books to read at home. I often checked out a library book, took it home and read it in one night, and returned it to the library the next day.

Atlanta High School competed with surrounding schools in football, basketball, and baseball, but football was king in Atlanta. The city supported the Rabbits football team, and they fared well against other schools, some with much larger student bodies. I was only fourteen years old when I graduated, so I was too small to go out for the school teams. In addition, I lived ten miles from school and was unable to practice sports after school. I stayed with my Aunt Bertha in Atlanta a few nights and practiced with the basketball team. I played briefly in one B team game, and that was it for my high school basketball career. I also played in one junior (fifteen years of age and below) softball game during my senior year. It sounds kind of strange for a high school senior to play on a junior team. I did not have an impressive sports resume when I graduated from high school; I do not recall any college scouts knocking on our door.

Although I did not play organized sports in Atlanta School, I did participate in various sports during recess, lunch time, and physical education classes. I played softball, basketball, and volleyball, but I never joined in the football games other than touch football. One of my few regrets about finishing high school so young was my inability to participate in school team sports. I played in a YMCA basketball league in Shreveport before I volunteered for the Air Force, however, and I played in a number of Air Force intramural basketball leagues during my four years in the Air Force.

I also failed to experience the normal high school social life. At fourteen, I had not discovered girls yet, so I missed out on the dating scene in high school. Also, a fourteen year old farm boy in the forties had little opportunity and not enough money to get involved with girls. I am happy to report, though, I did get up to speed in that phase of my life in my post-high school years. A big plus for finishing high school at fourteen years of age is class reunions. I am always the youngest one there, except for one or two spouses of classmates.

8.
The Country Church

R ural churches in my area of Cass County served multiple communities prior to World War II. Knight's Bluff, Antioch, and Blalock communities were home to three church buildings during that time period. Antioch Baptist Church, the largest church in the area, served worshipers within a four-mile radius. The Pentecost Church, relatively new in our area at the time, conducted services in the Old Liberty Church building prior to constructing their own facility about one-half mile from Antioch Baptist Church. The Old Liberty Church building remained vacant after the Pentecost congregation moved into their new quarters. An old Methodist Church building sat next to the Knight's Bluff schoolhouse, but it was unused most of the time. A Mormon Church congregation conducted services there periodically, and school or community social functions were held in the old Methodist Church building occasionally.

Antioch Baptist Church and the Pentecost Church were thus the only active congregations conducting regular worship services in the area during the time I was growing up. The Mormon congregation met occasionally in the Knight's Bluff schoolhouse, the old Methodist Church building, or in people's homes, but their membership was very small. Most members of the extended Hill family belonged to Antioch Baptist Church, so that is the church I grew up in. My parents visited the Pentecost Church during their revivals, and I remember going with Mother to Mormon services in the Knight's Bluff School once or twice.

Membership in rural churches was relatively small, and folks had very little money, so country churches were unable to hire staff. A part-time pastor was the only paid staff in most rural churches. Bi-vocational pastors normally served two congregations. They preached at one church on the first and third

Sundays each month, and they preached at a different church on the second and fourth Sundays. Pastors often resided outside the local area, hence they were unavailable at times other than the Sundays they were scheduled to preach. Congregations usually met for Bible study (Sunday School) on those Sundays the pastor was absent, and they conducted Wednesday night prayer meetings, either at church or in members' homes.

Farm folks in the thirties were God-fearing religious people, but they devoted minimal time to church. A lot of them lived several miles from their churches and did not have automobiles, so they either walked or rode in a wagon when they attended church. Farmers worked long hard hours six days a week, so Sunday was the only time they could visit family. Many rural folks, especially those without transportation, elected to visit parents or other family members on Sunday rather than go to church. Lack of money was another hindrance to regular church attendance. Many people, including my parents, believed they were obligated to contribute to the church financially when they attended services. If they did not have money to put in the offering plate, they did not go to church. Perhaps it was pride on their part, but it was their honest conviction.

We did not have a car until I was in high school, so my church attendance was irregular in my earlier years. We rode with someone, walked, or rode in a wagon on those Sundays we attended church. After Daddy bought our Ford Model T, we went to church regularly. The Antioch Church building was a plain wooden structure, typical of rural churches during that time period. The church had no electricity or running water, and we sat on long wooden pews without cushions. The church contained only two or three Sunday School rooms, so other classes met in different corners of the sanctuary for Bible study.

My recollection of Sunday School at Antioch Church is somewhat vague because I rarely participated. The women and most children attended Sunday School prior to the preaching service, whereas a lot of the men and older boys remained outside and visited during the Sunday School hour. Men worked hard in the fields all week with minimal contact with other people, so they looked forward to visiting with friends and neighbors on Sunday morning. And, the boys had to join in with the men.

One of my cousins, Harold, told me about an incident in Sunday School involving two other cousins. Edgar was sitting behind Bonnie and tied her dress strings to her chair. The teacher called on Bonnie to stand up and read, but she could not get out of her chair. Bonnie knew the guilty party, and she was more than a little displeased. Antioch Church did not feature indoor bathroom facilities, so the men and boys used the Antioch School outhouse across the road from the church. We went to a neighbor's well next to the school for drinking water.

I was barely fifteen years old when I moved away from home and stopped attending Antioch Baptist Church, so my spiritual perception of the church is limited. My views and recollections of Antioch Church are therefore those of a young teenager who had never faced up to his spiritual needs. At that time, I had not accepted Jesus Christ as my Savior and Lord. I was thus too young and spiritually immature to concentrate on the preaching, so I remember nothing about the pastor's messages. Two deacons always sat on the front row in front of the pulpit, and two or three kids usually stretched out on the pews asleep, yours truly included at times. A few of the adults also nodded off sometimes, no different from churches today. I recall one man in particular (I will call him Mr. Jones), one of our neighbors, who sat with his head back, his eyes closed, and his mouth open, oblivious to what the preacher was saying. I do not remember if Mr. Jones stood up for the invitation hymn or kept on snoozing.

Kids will be kids, so youngsters often acted up in church. A stern look or a sharp pinch from his or her mother usually ended the misbehavior, but if that did not work, one of the child's parents took the guilty party outside. There was no mistaking what took place outside the church. A good spanking always brought loud screams from the recipient of the spanking, so everyone knew the bad boy or girl was being punished for his or her "sins." In that particular instance, Jesus did not take on the punishment for the transgression of the naughty child. The child received the stripes himself. The pain and embarrassment of being taken outside served as an effective deterrent of future misbehavior.

We were often treated to special music in church. Two pretty twins, Doris and Dorothy, sang a lot of duets, and I remember Daddy singing tenor in a quartet special. Daddy joined three of my cousins, Clyde, Vaudine, and Mildred, to form a nice quartet. I recall Daddy singing regularly at home; one of his favorite songs was, "Rock of Ages." Our pastor preached at both the morning and evening services on Sunday. Bible study preceded the preaching service in the morning, and the church offered BTU (Baptist Training Union) prior to the evening sermon. I usually skipped Sunday School along with some of the men, but I attended BTU most of the time.

Church was a place for Bible study and worship, but we enjoyed fun-filled social activities as well. Dinner on the grounds was always a special treat. The ladies brought covered dishes, spread them out on tables in the shade of trees on the church grounds, and served everyone at the conclusion of the morning worship time. Those church dinners were times of good food and fellowship. The congregation recognized some of the ladies, including Mother, as very good cooks, so everyone tried to find out which dishes they brought so they could sample them.

Antioch Baptist Church provided occasional youth parties, with "youth" being any single person about twelve years of age and up. Those parties were held outside the church in the evening. Our church youth group included one or two couples who were enamored with one another, so our socials provided good settings for those couples to pursue that attraction. A lot of the games played at the youth parties included dark walks by couples around a short road loop adjacent to the church, so the guys had ample opportunities to hold their gals' hands and perhaps steal a kiss as they walked around the loop. I remember one youth party in particular. I was somewhat smitten by the pastor's daughter, and I jumped at the chance to stroll around the loop with her a couple of times. Unfortunately, I did not follow up on that pleasant encounter. Remember though, I was a country hick, not too cool socially.

Pie suppers were popular in the thirties and forties. We attended pie suppers at the old Methodist Church building in Knight's Bluff and at Antioch Baptist Church. I do not know if the pie suppers were school or church fund-raising functions, or perhaps both, but they were a lot of fun. The ladies baked pies to be auctioned off, and the man who bought a pie got to eat his pie with the lady who brought it. The bidding was quite competitive for pies baked by known good cooks. However, those pie suppers were rough on single guys whose girlfriends brought pies to be auctioned. A young lady expected her boyfriend to buy her pie, of course, but other men purposely bid the price of the pie to a high level. As a result, poor single guys, and sometimes newly married men, spent all their money buying their girlfriends' and wives' pies.

Church revivals were big events when I was growing up. Revivals were held in church buildings, in brush arbors, or out in the open on church grounds, and they usually lasted one or two weeks. The visiting evangelist preached a midday sermon and an evening sermon, and the pastor and evangelist ate meals with church members. Members of the church and other people in the surrounding communities attended revivals. My family participated in revivals at our own Baptist church, and we visited the Pentecost Church when they were in revival. During revivals, Antioch Baptist conducted Bible drills, presented special music, had Bible reading contests, and provided various other activities to create interest, especially among the young people. I recall reading dozens of chapters in the Bible each day during those Bible reading contests.

Not all my revival memories are pleasant. Before and after the daily sermons, the evangelist and pastor cornered various young people and tried to "save" them. I was taken aback by those high-pressure tactics, so I sometimes hid in the floorboard of our Model T to prevent the preachers from finding me. One or two of the older ladies also approached young people during the invitation hymns and tried to convince them to walk down the aisle and make a public profession of faith. Perhaps some young people were not bothered by those coercive tactics, but I felt very uncomfortable. That early church experience had a lasting impact on me. I accepted Jesus Christ as my Savior and Lord and made a public profession of faith many years later, just before my fiftieth birthday, and I did so with no coercion.

Pentecost revivals were substantially different from those in the Baptist church. The Pentecost Church was relatively new in the rural area where I lived, so my cousins and I had not been exposed to the charismatic worship style of the Pentecost denomination. Remember also that in our culture in the thirties, anything different was oftentimes looked on with disfavor. Baptist youth in particular did not understand and appreciate the outward expressions of praise and worship in the Pentecost revival services. We had not seen worshipers run up and down the aisle shouting, roll around and lie prone on the floor, raise hands and arms in prayer and praise, and speak in ecstatic tongues. As I recall, the Pentecost people referred to such outward expressions of worship as, "Seeking the Holy Ghost." Baptist youngsters found those actions strange, and kids being kids, we made fun of the charismatic worshipers. I remember times when my cousins and I played church and imitated folks in the Pentecost revival.

Rural churches did not contain baptisteries in those days. The pastor performed baptism by immersion in local rivers, streams, and lakes. I recall Antioch Baptist Church baptismal services at Mr. Harden's lake near the church. The pastor baptized new converts during warm weather, normally once a year, depending on the number of candidates for baptism. Antioch Church constructed a new building before I moved away from home. If I remember correctly, the decision to build a new church was somewhat controversial, as is the case for a large percentage of church building programs. I believe the bank providing the financing wanted key church members to cosign the note, but they refused. I do not know how that was resolved, but the church did build a new facility. The pastor and volunteers within the church accomplished a majority of the work. The work was done by amateur carpenters, so the quality of the building was probably questionable. I worked with Uncle Charlie and the pastor two or three weeks during one summer to help construct the new church.

Gospel singing schools were not part of the churches' agendas, but the schools involved church members and quite often church facilities. The Stamps-Baxter Music Company, founded in 1924, operated a music school and conducted singing schools across a broad area. A teacher, or leader, conducted a singing school in a community church or public school, and people from the surrounding area attended the school. Attendees included members of various churches in the area as well as folks with no church affiliation. I am not sure how the Stamps-Baxter Company and the singing schools were organized, but the leader for both the schools and other singing events in our part of the county lived in the area.

Stamps-Baxter conducted one of their singing schools at the Antioch Baptist Church around 1940. Men, women, and children from the Antioch, Knight's Bluff, Blalock, and Courtland communities attended the school, and the leader taught the basics of gospel singing. His instructions benefited both experienced and novice singers, and the school generated interest in gospel singing in the region. The teacher also led periodic one-day singing events at various locations in the area. My parents and a lot of our neighbors participated in those one-day singing sessions.

The Primitive Baptist Churches held three-day association meetings at various locations. Uncle Leonard, one of Daddy's brothers, was a pastor of two of their churches, so he and his family attended those meetings. Mother accompanied them to an association meeting in Arkansas one time, and I went with Mother to one of their tent meetings held in Queen City on the school grounds. I do not remember much of what transpired except for a lot of preaching. Harold, Uncle Leonard's son, and I spent most of the time on the school grounds away from the tent. We searched for discarded cigarette butts to smoke, a common practice for young boys back then.

Primitive Baptist churches were a little different from the Missionary Baptist Church at Antioch. All singing was a cappella; Primitive Baptist churches did not have musical instruments. Their churches were also somewhat smaller than Missionary Baptist churches. At one time, Uncle Leonard pastored three churches. He preached in one church twice each month, and he preached once each month in the other two. He spent fifth Sundays with his family, so my extended family planned special get-togethers on Uncle Leonard's off days.

My overall church experience as a youngster was very positive. Although I did not become a Christian until later in life, I gained Bible knowledge, learned Biblical principles for living, and observed Godly people living Godly lives. My parents strived to live good Christian lives, but they did not talk a lot about religion. Their actions spoke louder than their words. My parents' integrity, honesty, faithfulness, perseverance, generosity, compassion, and love for others demonstrated true Christian faith. Mother and Daddy were two of the Godly people I saw living Godly lives.

9.
A Resourceful and Creative Generation

Rural folks in the twenties and thirties worked family farms to provide for large families, and they did so with very little money. How did they do it? That generation's survival during the Great Depression is a testament of their fortitude, tenacity, resourcefulness, and creativity. My parents and their peers made do with what they had. They produced a vast majority of the goods they consumed with their hands, keeping purchases to an absolute minimum. Farmers and their families had roofs over their heads, clothing on their backs, and food for their stomachs, but not much else. They improvised in some areas, substituted in others, and did without in those areas in which they could not supply their own needs.

Most people in that time period owned their farms, although some were tenant farmers. They did not have mortgage payments, and few had electricity, running water, or telephones, so no one had utility bills to worry about. Folks did not carry home insurance, medical insurance, life insurance, or automobile insurance, so insurance premiums were not concerns for them. People paid cash for their cars, hence they had no car payments, and property taxes were negligible. Farmers therefore faced minimal ongoing expenditures for the land they farmed, the houses they lived in, and their transportation. Farmers' primary concern was to provide food and shelter for themselves and their farm animals as they planted, cultivated, and harvested crops to produce farm income. Rural folks struggled to generate sufficient farm income to sustain them through the next year's farming cycle.

The very nature of farming in the thirties enabled folks to eke out a meager living by the sweat of their brow. Farm equipment and implements were either manual or horse-drawn, and the initial cost for such farming tools was relatively low. Upkeep of hoes, shovels, plows, planters, disks, wagons, and other farm equipment was inexpensive, and each piece of equipment lasted many years. Farmers did their own maintenance on farm equipment, thus ongoing expenses for implements and equipment were negligible. Every farmer knew how to sharpen, adjust, tighten, lubricate, and maintain his farm tools, so his only farming expenses were for insecticides, fertilizers, and sustenance for his family and livestock.

Farmers saved seeds from year to year, hence seed costs were minimal. Seeds from one year's cotton, corn, peas, peanut, watermelon, cantaloupe, tomato, and potato harvest were saved to plant the following year's crops. Farmers bought inexpensive vegetable seeds and onion plants each year for their gardens. If for some reason a farmer had insufficient seeds to plant a crop, be borrowed seeds from a neighbor. Folks fertilized vegetable gardens and yard flowers with cow manure and chicken manure, so the only purchased fertilize was that for the fields. People occasionally bought inexpensive fertilize to spread on their pastures to enhance grass production.

Livestock and chicken feed was a significant expense, but farmers raised much of that feed to minimize those expenditures. And of course, the cattle and horses grazed on fertile pasture land. We raised peanuts and cut corn tops to provide hay for the cattle and horses, and we fed corn to the livestock, hogs, and chickens. Watermelons provided food for livestock, hogs, and chickens in season, and we fed table scraps, fruit peels, vegetable hulls, and various trimmings to the hogs and chickens. Folks did not waste any food; everything was recycled. We seldom bought dairy feed, but we did buy supplemental feed (shorts) for the hogs, and we purchased chicken feed to enhance egg production from the hens.

Meat was not a regular menu item when I was growing up. We butchered hogs in the winter, smoke-cured the hams and a portion of the hand-ground sausage, canned the remaining sausage in Mason jars, and packed what was left of the hog in a large wooden salt box for preservation. We ate fresh pork at hog-killing time and often had ham or sausage for breakfast the rest of the year. The pork packed in salt served primarily as seasoning for vegetables throughout the year. A staple for Sunday dinner was fried chicken, provided by one or two pullets taken from the chicken yard.

Rural folks ate little meat other than the pork and chicken they raised. Hunters and fishermen enjoyed squirrel, quail, and fish, but few people had time to hunt and fish; they were too busy with farm work. We ate fish occasionally when someone gave us a catfish or when Daddy bought one, and we considered fried catfish a real delicacy. Breakfast in our house consisted of homemade biscuits, fresh butter, ribbon cane syrup, canned preserves or jelly, coffee, and perhaps ham or sausage. We produced all breakfast items except coffee and flour to make the biscuits.

Dinner and supper meals were somewhat similar. We usually had two or three fresh or canned vegetables, biscuits and cornbread, Daddy's syrup, Mother's pickles or relish, milk or iced tea, a homemade dessert, and perhaps dried or canned fruit. We enjoyed fresh vegetables and fruit in season, along with tomatoes and cantaloupes, and we ate Mother's canned vegetables and fruit out of season. Mother made a lot of cakes, pies, fruit cobblers, puddings, fried fruit pies, and teacakes, so I developed a sweet tooth as a youngster. And, I have not lost that sweet tooth as of today; I must have my dessert with midday and evening meals.

Like breakfast, dinner and supper consisted primarily of things we produced. Mother bought flour, meal, sugar, salt, soda, baking powder, and spices, but virtually everything else she used in cooking was produced on the farm. Mother bought Mason jars, and occasionally new lids, but she reused the jars multiple times. Daddy took corn to a gristmill at times and had it ground into meal, so the expense for meal was eliminated. Mother often substituted farm-raised ribbon cane syrup for sugar in her desserts, so the expense for sugar was reduced. She did all cooking on a wood-burning stove, and we cut our stove wood from trees on the farm, so fuel for cooking cost nothing.

Helen, one of my cousins, remembers a time when her mother was in the middle of canning. Aunt Mildred needed some

Mason jar lids, so she sent her youngest sister, Alsiene, and Helen to Watkins Country Store for the lids. Aunt Mildred did not have any money, but she sent two dozen eggs to pay for the lids, a common practice in those days. The store was two miles away, so rather than walk, Alsiene and Helen decided to ride double on a horse. Helen sat behind Alsiene holding the bucket of eggs, and they were enjoying the ride.

Just before they reached the store, however, a log truck passed by and spooked the horse. The horse took off, and the bucket of eggs bounced up and down until Alsiene brought the horse under control. Guess what! Helen and Alsiene had a bucket of scrambled eggs when they reached the store. Mrs. Watkins gave Helen the Mason jar lids and told her Aunt Mildred could pay for them the next time she came in. Helen and Alsiene rode the two miles back home with the jar lids and their scrambled eggs.

Most farm folks ate well in the thirties, but as you can see, their food expenses were minimal. Everyone picked fruit from orchards, raised a variety of vegetables in gardens, and gathered wild berries and grapes from nearby woods and pastures, not necessarily their own. Ladies canned vegetables in Mason jars, canned or dried fruit, canned all kinds of jellies and preserves, made a variety of pickles and relishes, and stored onions and potatoes. A lot of ladies also made watermelon rind preserves, fig preserves, and sauerkraut; fig preserves and sauerkraut are still two of my favorite foods. Except for the cost of sugar, salt, spices, and mason jars, all that food was free; it was produced on the farm.

Housewives made soap by boiling a mixture of lye and hog fat in a wash pot. We used that lye soap to wash our hands, bathe, wash dishes, do laundry, and scrub floors, so we never purchased cleaning products. Lye soap was potent stuff, and it was harsh on the hands, but it was free. Mother washed our clothes in a No. 2 wash tub and boiled them in a wash pot, using only lye soap. She starched and ironed our clothes with irons heated on the cook stove, so the only cost of laundry was the minimal cost of starch.

Fertilize sacks and print feed sacks were the sources of a majority of the material used to make linens, quilts, dresses, and other articles of clothing. Chicken feed came in cotton print sacks, and women selected favorite print patterns to use in their sewing. They made dresses, blouses, shirts, and other articles of clothing and pieced quilts from those print sacks. Material scraps left over from making clothing were used to piece quilts. Print material scraps were highly valued; ladies hoarded those scraps and saved them in boxes for future quilting needs. Some brands of smoking tobacco came in small cotton bags. Housewives saved those tobacco sacks, dyed them, and used the dyed tobacco sacks in their quilts. Grandma Hill once pieced an entire quilt from dyed tobacco sacks.

Fertilize came in white cotton sacks with black letters. Women boiled the black letters out of those sacks and used them to make sheets, pillow cases, towels, wash cloths, slips, gowns, underwear, and other items of clothing. I cannot remember us buying kitchen, bathroom, or bedroom linens. We did not buy blankets or comforters either; we used homemade quilts for bed covers. Ladies made mattresses and pillows from either cotton or feathers, so we did not buy mattresses or pillows.

Houses and furnishings were plain, but the ladies appreciated nice things; they tried to feminize their homes as best they could. They crocheted and embroidered doilies, pillows cases, table scarves, and other items to decorate their homes. A few ladies crocheted table cloths and bedspreads, a huge undertaking. You are probably beginning to get the picture. Farm folks in the thirties did not buy anything they could make; they did not have the money.

I am sure you are wondering how country folks found time to do so much with so little. Well, they worked long hard hours, and the entire family pitched in to help. Kids did not play video games, watch television, surf the internet, text their friends, and hang out at the mall several hours each day; they toiled alongside their parents. People without funds faced a simple choice; you did without something you really needed, or you buckled down and improvised as best you could. Necessity without money breeds creative thinking, resourceful action, and perseverance. The alternative is helplessness and hopelessness.

Kids must have playthings. That is a truth for today's youngsters, and it was a truth for my generation. Our parents were unable to buy the toys we longed for and needed, but that yearning did not go away. We could have sulked, pouted, and felt miserable, but we chose to improvise and create our own playthings, and to do that, we had to persevere. I described in an earlier chapter how I made whistles, carved out toy guns, built stilts, constructed kites, laid out a basketball half-court, made a bat and ball, fashioned a slingshot, put up a Christmas tree, and made a bow and arrows. Those were not easy tasks for my peers and me, but we persisted and succeeded in supplying our own needs with the resources we had. Kids in my generation were happy and content in the midst of poverty.

Much of the furniture in farm houses was homemade. People lacked money to buy dining tables and chairs for large families, so they made their own. Few men were carpenters or cabinet makers, but they utilized their limited woodworking skills to construct plain wood dining tables with wood benches along the sides. They also made chairs, lamp tables, and other needed furniture items they were unable to purchase. A vast majority of farmers constructed their own barns, smokehouses, chicken houses, outhouses, and other farm structures. A lot of men built their homes as well, oftentimes with the aid of extended families and friends. And, they did all digging, sawing, hammering, trimming, sanding, and drilling manually.

Farm houses in the thirties featured wood-burning fireplaces or heaters and wood-burning cook stoves. Men and boys cut firewood and stove wood using two-man crosscut saws or one-man bow saws (pulp wood saws). Fences around fields and pastures incorporated barbed wire and wood posts. We cut the posts from small trees (saplings) and dug the postholes with a manual posthole digger. Daddy sharpened saws and other cutting tools with a hand file, and he replaced handles on hammers, axes, and other tools as needed. Nothing was easy without power equipment and power tools, but we made do with manual tools. Again, you play with the hand you are dealt.

Cotton was our money crop, but income was unpredictable as the result of fluctuating cotton prices, floods, droughts, boll weevils, and army worms. Even under ideal conditions, farmers were hard-pressed to make ends meet in the twenties and thirties, so they looked elsewhere for supplemental income. Men sawed logs, cut pulp wood, worked in sawmills, did construction work, worked for businesses in town, and worked on other jobs as much as possible, but temporary employment was difficult to find. They therefore turned to additional sources of revenue on their farms to help provide for their families.

My family kept two or three milk cows and a large flock of laying hens, so we had a good supply of milk and eggs. We churned milk, by hand of course, to obtain butter, and mother kept milk, butter, and cream cool by lowering it into our water well in buckets. She crated eggs and took them to town, along with milk, cream, and butter, and sold them to grocery stores and individuals. Daddy sold young steers and heifers, and sometimes older cows, to a buyer who took them to a livestock auction in a nearby town. We also sold fruit, vegetables, and watermelons occasionally to gain extra income. Such side income was minimal, but it was necessary to keep farm households afloat during those difficult Great Depression days.

Another of my cousins, Hubert, recalls the resourcefulness of his father, Uncle Creston. They had a larger than normal farm, Uncle Creston raised large quantities of sweet potatoes and Irish potatoes, and he stored them in a large potato house. He also raised a lot of melons, vegetables, and fruits. Uncle Creston would load up his wagon or car with produce and make a run to town. Regular customers, primarily African Americans, bought his produce on time payments, and they always paid him as promised. Uncle Creston usually collected enough on his runs to pay for the purchases he made while in town, with money left over. His produce business enabled Uncle Creston and his family to survive those difficult depression years.

Hubert and his brother, Troy, accompanied their father on shopping excursions to town, trips of several hours duration by wagon. Uncle Creston owned a Model T automobile, but he went shopping in a wagon. Hubert and Troy kept complaining about how slow the wagon was on one of those shopping trips. They wanted to know why they could not go in their car. Uncle

Creston finally told them, "Boys, I have corn to feed these mules, but I do not have money to buy gas." His answer reflects the economic condition and resourcefulness of farmers in the thirties.

A few men peddled the fish they caught, whereas others trapped raccoons and mink and sold the skins. Cass County was dry (no alcohol), so bootleg whiskey and homemade grape wine were in demand. Some of our neighbors responded to that demand by making and selling bootleg whiskey and wine. I recall watching federal agents (revenuers) fly over our area searching for whiskey stills. A few farmers raised and cured their own smoking and chewing tobacco rather than buy it. Times were very hard when I was growing up, and country folks looked for ways to save a buck or make a buck.

People on the farm had limited wardrobes. Two sets of everyday work clothes and a Sunday outfit were par for the course. Most school children also had two sets of school clothes. Sunday best for men and boys consisted of khaki pants, a nice shirt, and a decent pair of shoes. We wore overalls or jeans, a work shirt (or no shirt), brogan shoes (or no shoes), and a wide-brimmed straw hat to the fields. Boy's school clothes consisted of jeans or khaki pants, a seasonal shirt, and tennis shoes or loafers (or no shoes). Women patched clothes with snagged or worn holes; they did not discard them. In a like manner, men repaired or resoled worn out shoes rather than buy new ones.

Country folks often became ill or were injured, but they rarely went to a doctor. Farm households doctored themselves with home remedies, or the ailing person just toughed it out until his or her body healed itself if the illness was not serious. In the event of a serious sickness or injury, the family either contacted a doctor for a house call or took the patient to the doctor's office. Most people utilized popular over-the-counter medications such as castor oil, black draught, and Grove's Chill Tonic (a quinine tonic) to treat a variety of ailments. When kids were contrary or rambunctious, mothers lined them up and gave each a dose of castor oil to "work" the meanness out. Thank goodness, Mother's favorites were black draught and Grove's Chill Tonic, not nearly as harsh as castor oil.

Home remedies derived from various roots, bark, herbs, and leaves found in the woods were also popular. Grandma Hill made an ointment, "black salve," which was used to treat burns, cuts, thorns, teething babies, and other assorted ailments. Neighbors were always eager to purchase a can of her black salve after she made a fresh batch. I do not know what ingredients she used, but it was something found in nature, and folks had to have it.

Mother was the only person who knew the ingredients of that secret black salve recipe, because she was the one Grandma Hill sent into the woods to get what she needed for each batch. Mother and Grandma Hill went to their graves without divulging the ingredients for black salve, to the chagrin of our family. Grandma Hill also sent Daddy into the woods to fetch roots, bark, or leaves to make special teas for various sicknesses. People swore by those home remedies when I was growing up.

People back then believed certain individuals possessed unique powers to touch and pray over someone and heal them from specific ailments, for example burns or warts. I recall neighbors coming to Grandma Hill's house to have her reduce the pain or heal them from burns; she "talked" the pain away. I do not know if those healing powers possessed by a few individuals were real or imagined, but I experienced one such healing episode. As a young lad, my hands were covered with warts. A man Daddy knew rubbed my hands, and apparently prayed, and told me to forget about the warts. A short time later, perhaps days or weeks, all the warts were gone. Was that faith healing, or did the warts come off as a natural body process? I will not speculate, but I do know my warts disappeared.

Rural folks in my youth were uneducated for the most part and had little money, but they possessed what we called "horse sense" and a will to survive. They managed to feed and clothe their families during an extremely difficult time period. Their creativity, resourcefulness, tenacity, and perseverance enabled them to improvise and make good use of the resources available to them on the farm.

10.

Eking Out A Living

F armers in Northeast Texas and across the South struggled to make a living prior to the Great Depression, but their plight began a downward spiral on October 29, 1929, Black Tuesday. The stock market crashed, and people across our nation began a four-year run on banks. Thousands of farmers lost the little money they had in failed banks, and prices for farm products and timber plunged. A lot of farmers were unable to repay their bank loans, resulting in widespread foreclosures by banks. Almost one million farmers in our nation lost their family farms during the Great Depression, and those who survived faced precarious financial conditions.

The stock market crash in 1929 led to a steadily deteriorating economy over the next four years. The Dow Jones average dropped from 381 in September, 1929, to 42 in 1932. The nationwide unemployment rate shot up to twenty-five percent by 1933, and crop prices decreased sixty percent. Rural farming and logging industries were hardest hit in the early thirties, and a large number of men abandoned their families. Our country lacked government social programs to help people in need, so fifty percent of America's children lived with inadequate food, shelter, clothing, and medical care. Charities set up soup kitchens across our country to feed the hordes of unemployed and desperate people, and temporary housing provided shelter for some of those who lost their homes or were evicted. The few hired hands fortunate enough to find work on farms earned about two hundred dollars per year.

The Reconstruction Finance Corporation (RFC) established in 1932 under President Herbert Hoover provided some relief, distributing five billion dollars over three years. The RFC loaned money to large banks, railroads, farm mortgage associations, savings and loan associations, life insurance companies, and other big businesses. The RFC also provided aid to states and local governments, but little help filtered down to those on the bottom of the economic pyramid. The RFC was viewed as primarily a relief program for big business, with little help going to the working class. Trickle down economics does not work today and it did not work in 1932. Direct aid to hungry and desperate people was the medicine needed to pull America out of the Great Depression. Perhaps our federal and state governments should prescribe that same medicine to lift our country out of today's Great Recession.

Healing from the Great Depression began in 1933 under newly-elected President Franklin Roosevelt's New Deal. The Federal Emergency Relief Administration (FERA), the first relief program under the New Deal, was established in 1933. That program distributed three billion dollars over the next two years, with African Americans receiving a larger share. The Social Security Board took over FERA in 1935 when the Federal Deposit Insurance Corporation (FDIC) and Social Security were initiated. Prior to 1935, America had very little in the way of a social net. A form of Social Security was started in 1935 to help the elderly, some of the nation's most vulnerable citizens.

The Works Progress Administration (WPA), one of President Roosevelt's most effective New Deal agencies, was established in 1935, and it was renamed in 1939 as the Works Projects Administration. The WPA's main thrust was to provide employment on necessary government funded projects rather than on make-work tasks and direct relief. Relief was replaced by real jobs. The WPA funded a multitude of projects, including road and bridge construction, school and library construction, public parks and building construction, parks maintenance, day nursery work, Library of Congress research, and other blue-collar and white-collar jobs. WPA projects employed eight and one-half million workers between 1935 and 1943, usually at the prevailing local wages.

WPA employees worked thirty hours maximum per week on temporary jobs, earning between nineteen and ninety-four dollars per month. African Americans were again a large percentage of

WPA workers, and some workers ate and slept at the work sites. The agency distributed seven billion dollars between 1936 and 1939, including food and clothing to needy people. The WPA participated in defense work after the start of World War II, with forty percent of the workers assigned to defense jobs by the end of 1941. The WPA was discontinued in 1943 because of the ready availability of defense related jobs.

A similar New Deal program was the Emergency Conservation Work (ECW) program established in 1933, later renamed the Civilian Conservation Corps (CCC). That public works program focused on forestry, prevention of soil erosion, flood control, and other conservation issues. It involved natural resources conservation and development at the federal, state, county, and municipal levels. The CCC was a public work relief program for unemployed men to provide vocational training while performing useful work related to conservation and development of our nation's natural resources. The program provided near-term employment benefits as well as long-term financial payback. The CCC provided economic relief and vocational training for three million men between 1933 and 1942. Emphasis was switched from civilian endeavors to defense programs in 1939 and 1940.

CCC Road Construction in 1930s

I was too young to comprehend and remember much about the Great Depression or the New Deal programs established by President Roosevelt, but I do remember the lean times of the late thirties. I do not recall specific WPA projects, and I was not aware of extended family members or friends who worked for the WPA, but some did. Vaudine, one of my older cousins, tells me she worked on several short-term government projects during that time period. Her brother, Clyde, was employed on a CCC project in Arizona where he learned the brick mason trade. That training and experience as a brick mason served Clyde well for many years.

The suppressed prices of farm products, especially cotton, were probably the most significant impact of the Great Depression on my immediate family. I do not recall any of our extended family or neighbors losing family farms to bank foreclosures, but it most likely happened. Daddy worked a tenant farm, did not own a car, and had to provide for a family of only three, so his load was much lighter than that of most of his peers who supported households numbering six or more.

We raised virtually everything we ate, made a majority of the household goods we used, raised most of our livestock feed, and made some of the clothes we wore. The federal government distributed food commodities to needy families, but my parents refused those relief handouts. We did without the things we could not produce and were unable to purchase. Most people I knew had ample food on the table because they raised it, fished for it, hunted it, or received government relief commodities. They also had shelter, although some of their houses were barely livable, but clothing was another story. A lot of folks, particularly those with large families, relied on extended families or neighbors for hand-me-down clothes. People helped one another.

I did not realize it at the time, but some of my neighbors, and perhaps members of my extended family, were possibly among the fifty percent of children who did not have adequate food, shelter, clothing, and medical care in the thirties. I was exposed to only the people who lived near us, and I was too young to keep up with news reports, but I am sure our area was typical of the rural South. Daddy was able to keep us afloat financially, but some of our neighbors were probably not as fortunate, especially those with large families. All rural folks, as well as a majority of city dwellers, sacrificed, did without necessities, and earned extra income any way they could. Farming simply did not provide a livable income during the Great Depression years.

Cotton was the primary money crop in our area of Northeast Texas, but farm families sold dairy products, eggs, fruits, vegetables, watermelons, and livestock to earn a supplemental income. Men also worked in sawmills, sawed logs, cut pulp wood, worked in construction, worked in lumber yards, and worked in gas stations, but those jobs were scarce in the thirties. I recall Daddy sawing logs for a few months one year. He rode on a company truck with several other men to the work site near Texarkana. Two men cut the logs with a crosscut saw and an axe, and they were paid according to the feet of logs they cut; the two men split the earnings. But, Daddy was paired with a one-armed man who was unable to pull his share of the load on the crosscut saw, and he could not trim off large limbs with the axe. Daddy thus did a majority of the work but received only one-half the pay. He did not complain, though, because he did not want to cheat the one-arm man; that is just the way Daddy was.

A canning plant in Atlanta provided seasonal work for ladies. Vaudine, one of my older cousins, worked for a time in the canning plant peeling tomatoes. She earned a whopping five cents per bucket of tomatoes peeled, and she was happy to get the work. I remember an interesting story about the canning plant. The story goes that workers put peeled tomatoes in one bucket and peelings in another. The company made tomato ketchup from the peelings, but women who dipped snuff spit in the peelings bucket. I do not know if the story was true, but I do know a majority of women dipped snuff in those days. Readers, do not let that story come to mind the next time you squirt ketchup on your French fries.

Vaudine also tells of her first job after graduating from high school. She applied for a job with Lovelady's Variety Store, but she had no sales experience. The owner informed her he could not hire an inexperienced sales clerk, but Vaudine did not give up. Determined to land that job, she asked if she could work for free to gain experience. The owner agreed to her offer, so Vaudine worked for a time with no pay. She demonstrated she could do the job, and the owner hired her for one dollar per day. A dollar a day sounds low now, but a dollar was a lot of money for a country girl in the thirties.

Vaudine's story reminds me of my first job a few months after graduating from high school in 1947. I was barely fifteen years old and was unable to work in a factory type job because of child labor laws. I settled for a soda jerk job in Walker Drug Store in Atlanta. I knew nothing about milk shakes, malts, sundaes, fountain drinks, floats, or banana splits. My experience with ice cream was limited to Dixie Cups, ice cream cones, and homemade ice cream, but Mr. Walker trained me. To him, I was always Butch. I quickly learned the soda jerk trade, and I also sold goods all over the store and made home deliveries on a one-speed bicycle. I worked six ten-hour days per week for fifteen dollars, a lot of money for a hick from the sticks. At twenty-five cents per hour, you can see that the pay scale for retail store employees did not increase that much from the thirties to the forties.

Employment opportunities in Northeast Texas were very limited until 1941 when the Japanese bombed Pearl Harbor. After that, government defense spending lifted the economy. Two major defense plants provided good-paying jobs in the Ark-La-Tex region after America entered the war. The federal government purchased over one hundred farms and ranches near Texarkana, occupying in excess of fifteen thousand acres. Construction of both the Lone Star Army Ammunition Plant and the Red River Army Depot (RRAD) started in late-1941. Those huge facilities provided jobs for several thousand workers, first in clearing the land and construction of the many buildings, and then in operating the plants. Daddy quit farming temporarily to help clear land for the Lone Star plant.

The Lone Star AAP was adjacent to the RRAD, about eleven miles from the city of Texarkana. Military activities in both facilities began in 1942. The Lone Star plant manufactured military ammunition of various types, whereas the Red River facility stored and shipped the munitions produced by the Lone

Star plant. RRAD also trained military personnel in use of the munitions. The two plants were combined in 1945 and renamed the Red River Arsenal. That facility operated continuously until the present time, and it is also used now as a major maintenance depot, especially for Bradley vehicles. Both my parents and many of our neighbors worked in the Lone Star and Red River defense plants during Word War II, and a lot of them remained with Red River Arsenal in subsequent years.

Daddy's youngest sister and Edgar's mother, Aunt Cora, remained with the Lone Star plant many years after World War II. She retired from the defense plant and lived on her family farm where Edgar was born until her death at one hundred and five years of age. Aunt Cora lived by herself and did a lot of her own cooking until the time of her death. Hard work, visits from family, fried chicken, coconut cake, and periodic glasses of wine kept her going all those years. And, she was spry and alert right up to the end. I hope I have some of her genes.

Life was difficult for rural folks in the twenties, but farmers really struggled to survive during the Great Depression years of the thirties. World War II brought economic relief to our country in the forties, but at the cost of the lives of hundreds of thousands of our young men in the military. Many rural people cut back on farm activities to work in defense related jobs or serve in the military. As a result, women had to step up to the plate and fill jobs previously held by men. In addition to defense plant work, women ran retail stores, worked in factories and warehouses, held down office jobs, kept the farms going, and worked in various other jobs. Word War II was thus a major factor in advancing the role of women in the workplace.

11.
Racism and Discrimination

R acial, ethnic, and religious discrimination has plagued our world for centuries, and America joined in that inhuman global practice. Protestant Christians in our country condemn Catholics in Europe for murdering thousands of so-called heretics during the Inquisitions of the Middle Ages. And, Americans condemn Hitler and fascist Germany for slaughtering six million Jews during the Holocaust. Religious wars, ethnic cleansing, racial genocide, and religious Jihad account for an overwhelming majority of the violence and strife around our world.

What is America's history regarding racial and ethnic discrimination? We like to think we are better than the rest of the world, but are we? Early settlers of our country slaughtered thousands of Native Americans and confiscated their lands. Our country signed treaties with those Native Americans, but we broke the treaties and took back the lands we gave them. Even today, a majority of our Native American population lives on reservations located in the least-desirable regions of our country. Native Americans today are burdened with virtually the same living conditions I experienced seventy years ago. They reside in the midst of a modern high-tech society but are relegated to reservations reminiscent of rural America in the thirties and forties.

I participated in a church mission trip to the Navajo reservation in the four corners region of New Mexico about five years ago. That was my first exposure to the Native American culture, and I was appalled at their living conditions. Two hundred thousand Navajo citizens live in a rugged and desolate area about the size of West Virginia. They are scattered across the countryside, most without decent roads (or with no roads) to their houses. Less than one-half the Navajos have electricity and running water, and the unemployment rate is about fifty percent. Their primary occupation is sheep herding, but the land is too poor to support its occupants, so the Navajos rely to a great extent on government aid for survival. Those dirt-poor people live in small dilapidated shacks or Navajo Hogans with dirt floors, and most use coal or wood burning heaters. A few Navajos leave the reservation and blend in with the modern world, but most remain on the reservation and continue in the poverty of their parents.

Even more tragic than America's treatment of Native Americans is our shameful treatment of African Americans. Slavery in our country was started in colonial America when natives from Africa were brought to our shores and sold as slaves. Slave labor was used primarily in agriculture, especially on cotton and tobacco plantations. Black people were considered as property; they had no rights, and many were physically abused. Both Christians and non-Christians were slave owners, and about one-half our nation's households owned slaves. African Americans were relegated to rundown shacks, all were forced to do hard manual labor, men were beaten, young girls were raped, and they had no legal rights.

Four million black slaves were freed in 1865, but cruel discrimination against African Americans continued for many years, especially in the South. The poll tax and accompanying literacy tests prevented most black people from voting, and the Ku Klux Klan (KKK) terrorized African American neighborhoods well into the Twentieth Century. Institutional racism, legal discrimination, and racial segregation were widespread until the late 1900s. The civil rights movement was initiated in the thirties; racial discrimination in the defense industry was banned by President Roosevelt in 1941; President Harry Truman integrated the military forces in 1948; and public schools were desegregated in 1954. Civil rights laws passed under President Lyndon Johnson in 1964 granted far-reaching rights and opportunities to people of color, but significant racial bias and discrimination remain even today. So, America owns a shameful history of prejudice and discrimination against minority segments of our population.

I grew up in the backdrop of that racial discrimination, but bias against African Americans was only a part of our overall prejudices. Folks in my neck of the woods were intolerant of anyone "different." We were prejudiced against Catholics, Jews, Mexicans, and Gypsies, as well as African Americans. I obviously grew up in a white Protestant locality, typical of thousands of other rural communities across the South. Our attitude toward, and treatment of, African Americans thus mirrored that of similar rural communities and was consistent with the racial biases of our nation as a whole.

I pointed out previously that Knight's Bluff community was all-white in the thirties, but a lot of African Americans resided in surrounding communities and in the cities of Queen City and Atlanta. A few farmers, including two of my uncles, housed black families on their farms. Those families lived in small separate shacks and helped with the farm work. It is my understanding that African American families worked on salaries rather than as share croppers. Other farmers hired African Americans to help plant, cultivate, and harvest their crops, paying them the prevailing wages at the time.

To be absolutely honest, white folks considered black people as second-class citizens when I was growing up. Slavery was a policy of the past, and a majority of the people I knew did not mistreat or abuse African Americans, but white people clearly treated them as an inferior race. A relatively small percentage of Caucasians did physically abuse and take advantage of black people, however. I remember two or three white men boasting about tying their African American workers to trees and whipping them with horse whips. True or not, that was an attitude with which some of our neighbors viewed black people. My parents and extended family were fair and just in dealings with individual African Americans as far as I know, but a lack of respect for the black race in general was evident.

We were no different from people throughout the South, and perhaps the entire country. My parents and a majority of their peers were kind and considerate to African American hired help and acquaintances, but at the same time they walked in lockstep with a society which suppressed and oppressed the black race.

Few black people owned the farms they worked, and their ramshackle houses were inferior to those of their white neighbors. Rural communities and cities were segregated. African Americans resided in separate areas of rural communities and in clearly defined sections of cities. For example, the black population of Atlanta in the thirties was concentrated in a rundown part of town designated by a racially-offensive name I will not repeat.

I do not remember a rural African American school near us, although there was a black school in Antioch community. It was located in the midst of a black settlement not too far from the Caucasian school. I have no knowledge of that black school, and I do not know what percentage of African American children attended school. However, I suspect a large percentage of them never attended school, and of those who did, few finished elementary school.

The Queen City School District was segregated, with an African American school located a short distance from a larger and much nicer Caucasian school. The two schools were in sight of each other, or in hollering distance as we said back then, but white kids did not interact with black kids. I was not aware of a school bus service for rural African Americans, and bus routes to the Queen City Caucasian school served only white kids. A few white children dropped out of school at a young age, and I am sure chronic absenteeism was the norm in the black community. African American neighborhoods, houses, and schools were clearly inferior to those of white folks.

A majority of public facilities were segregated when I was a youth. Restrooms and water fountains were designated as "white" and "colored," and waiting rooms in bus stations and train stations were segregated. African Americans sat in the back of buses, often standing up with empty seats in the front white sections. A lot of restaurants and cafes refused to serve black customers, and those few who did provided separate dining areas. A large number of businesses also required African Americans to use back doors rather than front entrances. In every area of the thirties' society, black folks were expected to stand back and allow white people to go first. I am sorry to say I grew up with, and was a part of, that selfish and shameful mindset.

Colored Water Fountain

Colored Bus Waiting Room

African Americans gained the right to vote at the conclusion of the Civil War, but few voted for many years, especially in Southern states. Most Southern states established the poll tax and literacy tests to suppress the black vote. A disproportionate number of African Americans were poor and could not afford the poll tax. In addition, a majority of black folks were uneducated and thus could not pass biased literacy tests designed to weed them out. The poll tax and literacy tests were eliminated in 1964, but barriers for African American voting remained.

A lot of unscrupulous employers of African Americans, together with the KKK, intimidated black people and prevented them from voting. Other employers paid the poll taxes for their black employees, transported them to voting places, and required them to vote for designated candidates. Even today, black voter turnout is substantially lower than that of their white counterparts, and rigged redistricting by states reduces the impact of minority votes. The Fifteenth Amendment to the Constitution, ratified in 1870, eliminated race as a criteria for voting. Yet, black people faced significant barriers to voting seventy years later when I was a youth, and they still face barriers in 2010.

You would think churches are the least likely places to be segregated, but that is not the case. In fact, some churches and denominations led the way in maintaining slavery in America and in suppressing black voter turnout. It has been said that eleven o'clock Sunday morning is the most segregated time in our country. Integration of our churches is taking place gradually, but a large percentage of minority segments of our population prefer their own churches and their particular worship styles. Also, a lot of white churches still do not welcome minority members, especially African Americans. Racial prejudice is alive and well in a lot of our churches.

Racial segregation in the armed forces of our country was discontinued in 1948, and I volunteered for the Air Force in 1951. It was then that I realized I was a Southern racist and began to change my attitude toward African Americans and other minorities. That breaking away from my Southern roots was a slow process which continued through four years in the military, four years in college, seventeen years in electrical engineering, and twenty-two years as a retail business owner. I still tend to stereotype people at times on the basis of race, ethnicity, and religion, but I strive to suppress that bias.

12.
World War II

The Great Depression of the thirties came to an abrupt end with the advent of World War II. Federal spending on defense and the military lifted our country out of the economic pit of the Great Depression. Government demand for all types of products snowballed, millions of defense related jobs opened up, military enlistments shot up, workers' wages ramped up, the bottom dropped out of unemployment, and prices for consumer goods surged. Government intervention and tight control kept the economy on a sustainable path and ensured an adequate supply of commodities to meet the country's burgeoning military and defense needs. But, World War II exacted a terrible price from our nation, the lives of over four hundred thousand of our brave soldiers.

Hitler's fascist Germany invaded Poland in 1939 to start the war that would end all wars. Germany and its ally, Italy, proceeded to conquer the European nations, one by one, over the next two years. Our nation required all men over twenty-one years of age to register for the draft in June, 1941, and Germany fired on the first U.S. warship in September of that year. Japan bombed Pearl Harbor three months later on December 7, 1941, inflicting heavy damage to our naval forces. Congress declared war against Japan, Germany, and Italy within the next few days, and the battle was on for U.S. military forces. Japan had awakened a "sleeping giant."

The U.S. economy shifted to war production by 1941. Japanese forces disrupted our nation's foreign supply of steel, oil, rubber, tin, sugar, coffee, and other products, and scarcity of transport ships further reduced availability of those products. Automobile manufacturing plants switched to production of military vehicles, with new car manufacturing banned in 1942.

Liquor disappeared from store shelves by 1944 as distilleries produced alcohol for wartime use, and one-third of our cigarette production was allocated to the military. The military gave our soldiers free cigarettes in World War II, leading to a surge in tobacco addiction in our country. The increasing government demand for all kinds of products, together with supply shortages, led to large price increases, and then rationing, for most consumer goods. The government began rationing consumer products in early 1942 and froze prices on consumer goods in May of that year.

The federal government began construction of huge defense plants to produce munitions and equipment for the military, and existing manufacturing facilities were converted from manufacture of consumer goods to production of military equipment and supplies. As a result, millions of high-paying jobs opened up. Those defense related operations absorbed workers from Works Projects Administration (WPA) programs, brought the nationwide unemployment rate down, and raised workers' pay scales. Hundreds of thousands of young men volunteered or were drafted for military service, further reducing the number of job seekers. World War II thus pumped up our overall economy and ended the Great Depression.

World War II ushered in fundamental changes to rural America. Millions of farmers abandoned or cut back on their farming operations to pursue more lucrative defense related work. Higher paychecks enabled people to purchase more consumer goods, thus raising rural folks' overall standard of living. Farm households no longer produced a majority of the goods they consumed; they had money in their pockets to purchase things they had previously done without. The entire face of wartime America changed, but transformations in rural life were more evident than changes for urban dwellers.

Northeast Texas was typical of other rural areas in our nation. The government constructed the Lone Star Army Ammunition Plant and the Red River Army Depot, both near Texarkana, in 1941. Those two giant defense plants supplied thousands of jobs during the war, and they were later combined and continue to operate today. My parents worked in those defense plants during the war, as did a large number of our neighbors. People commuted in carpools during those war years, and my parents saved enough of their earnings to purchase a car and their own farm after the war. They left their tenant farm behind, and we had transportation to church, to visit family, and for shopping in Queen City and Atlanta. Word War II definitely raised our standard of living.

Few women worked outside the home prior to the war, especially in rural areas. Relatively high paying defense work enticed millions of women to join the labor force. In addition, millions of men left the civilian workforce to serve in the military, creating a huge void in the male labor pool of our country. Women stepped up to the plate and filled jobs normally staffed by men. Women worked in defense plant jobs, and they also managed retail establishments, labored in warehouses, ran offices, worked in banks and insurance companies, performed all kinds of factory work, filled mechanic jobs, worked in other jobs away from the farm, and managed family farm operations. Those second salaries enhanced families' ability to purchase a wide range of consumer products, again raising their standard of living. World War II forever changed the gender mix of America's labor force.

Military service in the forties was a far cry from service in the high-tech military of today. Recruits went through a few weeks of basic training, rode troop rail cars to points of departure, boarded troop transport ships bound for European or Pacific war zones, and joined the battles. I recall watching troop trains loaded with soldiers pass through Atlanta. Hopeful soldiers threw pieces of paper containing their names and mailing addresses to teenage girls standing by the tracks, asking the girls to write them. In that foot soldier war, a young warrior's basic requirement was the ability to fire a rifle accurately and dig a foxhole quickly. Enemy lines at point-blank range and close-proximity combat in World War II resulted in heavy casualties on both sides. America suffered over four hundred thousand military deaths in the war, but the military toll for Germany, Japan, Russia, and China was measured in the millions.

Few American families remained untouched by the huge loss of life in the war. The draft near the end of the war encompassed men from eighteen to thirty-eight years of age, so Daddy was too old to serve and I was too young. But, our family was touched by the carnage. One of my first cousins, Troy, was killed in Europe a few short months after his wedding and enlistment, and his wife's brother, and our close neighbor, also died in battle. Several of my uncles and cousins went to war for our country, as did a lot of our neighbors. A few unlucky young men were classified 4-F, unfit for military service due to physical problems. They endured snide remarks and hostility from folks who had loved ones in the military. Being classified 4-F by the draft board was not a badge of honor in those days.

Families back home waited weeks at times for letters from soldiers abroad. Overseas telephone calls, Emails, and video hookups were technologies of the future, so the only communication between soldiers and their loved ones was by letter, and mail was transported by ship; it really was snail mail back then. I remember wives and mothers anxiously awaiting overdue letters from their soldiers serving in war zones, and I am sure the soldiers were just as anxious for letters from home. Mail was often slow in catching up with soldiers on the move, or involved in heavy fighting, so their letters arrived in batches at times. And, in the heat of battle, our troops found it difficult to write and send letters to loved ones.

We did not have nightly television news reports to keep us informed regarding daily happenings on the war fronts. Folks in my rural community did not receive daily newspapers, so we relied on radio news broadcasts for updates on the war, and that news was not always current. Imbedded journalists and war correspondents such as well-known Ernie Pyle provided most of the reports from the battle zones. Ernie Pyle reported on the war from Europe, Africa, and the Pacific region before he was killed by the Japanese during our invasion of Okinawa in 1945. Ernie Pyle wrote from the perspective of the common foot soldier, and his reports were carried by three hundred newspapers. He was instrumental in getting Congress to pass "The Ernie Pyle Bill" which gave infantrymen an extra ten dollars combat pay per month.

The United States rationed a wide variety of consumer commodities, starting in 1942 and ending in 1945 when supplies were sufficient to meet demand. Sugar rationing continued, however, until 1947, two years after the war ended. Hundreds of manufacturing facilities converted from production of consumer goods and equipment to manufacture of military parts and equipment. Virtually all products derived from rubber, steel, oil, iron, tin, kerosene, meat, and sugar were in short supply. Rationed items included farm equipment, bicycles, stoves, typewriters, office equipment, automobile tires and tubes, rubber goods, shoes, canned goods, meat products, cigarettes, coffee, sugar, gasoline, fuel oil, cheese, and foods made with sugar, among others.

Eggs, dairy products, canned turkey, and canned chicken were among the few commodities not rationed. The government encouraged people to utilize substitutes for rationed goods. Folks used cottage cheese and dried beans as meat substitutes, oleomargarine to replace butter, and saccharin or syrup instead of sugar. Actually, widespread use of saccharin as a sugar substitute began during World War I. Women developed a wide range of recipes which did not require rationed products. The government also urged people to plant vegetable gardens, or Victory Gardens, to produce much of their food. Our country put in place nationwide practices to conserve critical commodities, but rural farm folks routinely implemented a lot of those measures as a normal way of life. We raised our meat and vegetables, canned fruits and vegetables in Mason jars, produced our poultry and dairy products, and used saccharin and home-produced syrup instead of sugar.

Gasoline rationing was probably the most difficult issue to deal with during the war. Our government issued gas coupons to limit the purchase of gasoline for automobiles. Our country classified cars and trucks according to their use, and stickers placed on the vehicles indicated their use. One-half the automobiles nationwide were classified as unessential, and each vehicle received an A sticker. Four gallons of gas per week were allowed for those A sticker cars. Vehicles used for commuting or commercial purposes received different stickers (B, C, or D), and they were allocated larger amounts of gasoline. Gas rationing did not affect my family and our neighbors that much. Some did not own cars, and no one drove a lot except people commuting to work, and they received a higher gasoline allocation. A sizeable number of the folks commuting to defense plant jobs in Texarkana car-pooled to reduce expenses and to conserve gasoline.

Rubber was another commodity in short supply, and a large percentage of available rubber was allocated to the defense industry and the military. Consumers therefore faced rationing of tires, shoes, rubber footwear, and other rubber goods. Our government initiated a national "Victory Speed" of thirty-five miles per hour on our roadways, primarily to extend the life of automobile tires rather than to conserve gasoline. Rationing of rubber goods did not affect rural farmers a great deal. Our manual farm equipment did not utilize rubber tires, few farmers owned tractors, we did not drive our cars great distances, and we purchased minimal footwear. Again, those folks commuting to jobs were allowed to buy additional tires and tubes.

Steel, iron, and tin were also scarce during the war, and a large portion of available metal was used to produce military equipment. Manufacture of automobiles, farm equipment, bicycles, typewriters, stoves, heaters, office equipment, tools, and other metal goods was curtailed during the war. Our nation encouraged people to salvage and save scrap metal and bring it in for recycling. I remember searching for and saving broken or worn out farm implements and taking them to school during scrap metal drives. Shortages of farm implements and equipment, stoves and heaters, wagons, tools, pots and pans, and other metal goods did not pose a significant problem for us because those items usually lasted quite a few years. We were able to obtain or repair essential goods in spite of metal shortages.

Sugar rationing did pose a problem for ladies on the farm. Everyone canned vegetables, fruits, preserves, and jellies, and sugar was a necessary ingredient for those items. Mother used saccharin instead of sugar for iced tea sweetener, and she substituted syrup for sugar in a lot of her baking, so she was able to hoard her sugar allotment for use in canning. Ladies occasionally wound up with more sugar than they needed, so they gave it to neighbors who did not have enough. Sugar was a precious commodity during the war, and people used it sparingly.

Sugar shortages affected me and millions of other kids directly. Candy was in short supply in grocery stores, especially choice candy bars such as Baby Ruth and Butterfinger. Gilley's General Store kept their stock of candy under the counter and rationed it out to better customers. I fondly recall Mrs. Gilley giving Mother one or two of those choice candy bars from under the counter during our weekly shopping trips to Queen City and Atlanta. I do not remember any particular difficulty in getting ice cream cones and Dixie Cups, but perhaps they were scarce as well.

The government issued ration books containing coupons to each American family, and folks used those coupons to buy rationed commodities. Unscrupulous people stole ration coupons as well as rationed goods, and others printed counterfeit ration books. Rationed goods were priced at two levels, the one set by government controls and the price charged on the black market. A few crooked retailers sold scarce goods for prices higher than those set by the government. Black market selling flourished during the war. Human nature has not changed. You can always find a few folks who take advantage of other people's woes and milk the system for obscene profits, either legally or illegally.

Our nation sold war savings bonds and stamps to finance World War II. The government introduced Series E bonds in 1941, and those bonds' face value was twenty-five dollars and up. People bought the bonds for seventy-five percent of their face value and redeemed them ten years later for their face value. Folks scrimped and saved to buy savings stamps, and they pasted them in books. Once the books were full, people traded them in for war bonds. Folks sacrificed in the forties to support our military. Men and a few women from all walks of life served in the armed forces; everyone did without scarce consumer goods and conserved critical commodities; and people from all economic levels sacrificed to buy war bonds. Unlike recent wars in Iraq and Afghanistan, citizens from all walks of life and all economic levels shared the pain and sacrifice of World War II.

Education level and particular skills were not prerequisites for military service, and deferments were rare during World War II. Doctors, lawyers, sons of wealthy families, salesmen, farmers, bankers, sports and movie stars, factory workers, and men from all economic levels shared the same foxholes. And, all their families shared in the anguish of receiving a visit from a military officer informing them of the death of their soldier. People did not complain about paying taxes to support our troops, and few tried to shirk their personal responsibility to pay their fair share. Furthermore, our government did not borrow huge sums of money from foreign countries to finance the war.

Our government asked ordinary citizens like you and me to buy war bonds, and the people responded. Everyone sacrificed and did their part, unlike selfish and self-serving Americans today who place the burden and the sacrifices of the wars in Iraq and Afghanistan on our troops and their families and pass the costs of war to their children and grandchildren. Patriotism is not wearing a flag lapel pin and a "Support Our Troops" decal on a car bumper while sending a neighbor's son or daughter off to war. True patriotism is sending one's own son or daughter to fight, paying one's fair share in taxes to pay for a war worth fighting, and doing what is best for our country rather than what is best for self. Somehow, true patriotism seems to have taken a back seat to selfishness, greed, and self-gratification over the last seventy years.

President Roosevelt died in April, 1945, and Vice-President Harry Truman took office as President and Commander-in-Chief. Germany surrendered to the Allied Forces the next month, but Japan continued to fight. The Enola Gay bomber dropped mankind's first atomic bomb on the Japanese city of Hiroshima on August 6, 1945, and a second bomb was dropped on the city of Nagasaki three days later. The death tolls in Hiroshima and Nagasaki were 140,000 and 80,000, respectively. Japan formally surrendered on the deck of the USS Missouri on September 2, 1945, and World War II was over.

Nagasaki Atomic Bomb Mushroom Cloud

Enola Gay B-29 Bomber

An important legacy of the war was the G.I. Bill of Rights which had a profound impact on Americans' way of life. President Truman signed the Servicemen's Adjustment Act, or G.I. Bill, into law in 1944. It included provisions for aid to wartime veterans for college or vocational training and for zero-down low-interest home loans. By 1956 when the original G.I. Bill expired, 7,800,000 World War II veterans participated in education and training, and 2,400,000 veterans obtained Veteran's Administration (VA) home loans. The original G.I. Bill was replaced by the broader Montgomery G.I. Bill to cover veterans in later wars. I went to college from 1955 to 1959 under the G.I. Bill and purchased my first home with a VA loan in 1959.

Prior to World War II, few rural male high school graduates attended college. In addition to the millions of veterans who attended college under the G.I. Bill, large numbers of non-veteran high school graduates elected to attend schools of higher learning. The result was a highly educated workforce in America, increased worker salaries, and a higher standard of living for everyone. VA loans enabled millions of veterans to realize the American dream of "owning your own home." And, higher worker salaries contributed to additional increases in home ownership, as well as purchases of automobiles, appliances, furniture, and other consumer goods. The G.I. Bill thus changed the economic landscape of our nation.

Women in huge numbers joined the workforce during the war, and a lot of them did not return home fulltime at the war's end. Those second salaries provided economic strength in American households, and the increased disposable incomes led to purchases of luxury items previously unaffordable for most folks. Farm families built nicer homes, bought new cars, added electricity and running water to their homes, and splurged on televisions, boats, and other non-essential consumer goods. Unfortunately, that enhanced affluence of American households did not lead to more secure and stable marriages. Broken families and divorce rates increased as family wealth increased, and that family instability is even more pronounced today.

World War II and all of its ramifications changed the face of rural America, but those changes came at a great cost, the lives of four hundred thousand of our soldiers.

13.
Reflection on the Past

The Hill family as I know it originated in the Carolinas, moved to Tennessee, and later migrated to Texas. William Hill, my great-great-grandfather, was born in South Carolina in 1792, and he married Jane Cole, born in North Carolina in 1791. They had ten children while living in Tennessee, the youngest being Holden Lafayette Hill, my great-grandfather, born in 1834. The family moved to Cass County, Texas, at some time prior to 1854. Martha Elizabeth Dobbs, my great-grandmother, was born in Alabama in 1835, and she traveled by ox wagon with her family to Texas in 1841. Her father, Cyrus Dobbs, was buried in the Old Liberty Cemetery in Antioch community, and I believe he was the first person buried there. Holden Lafayette Hill married Martha Elizabeth Dobbs in 1854, and to that union was born four children, including William Lafayette Hill, my grandfather.

My great-grandfather died in the Civil War, and his wife never remarried. William Lafayette Hill married Clemmie Victoria Frazier in 1889, and they had eight children, including Jasper Grayden Hill, my father. He married Mora Esther Brown, daughter of James Tandy Brown and Alma Victoria Brown in 1929, and I came into this world in 1932. Grandpa Hill and Grandma Hill raised their family on a farm in Antioch community, ten miles from Atlanta, Texas.

The Brown family migrated from North Carolina to Cass County, Texas, in the early 1800s. William Weekly Brown, my great-great-great-grandfather, was born in North Carolina in 1825, and he moved to Cass County prior to 1849. His son, and my great-great-grandfather, Tandy B. Brown, was born in 1849. He married Martha Elizabeth Clements, and they had a son, Dewrell Weatherford Brown, my great-grandfather. Dewrell

Weatherford Brown married Louella Ann Tally, and to that union was born my grandfather, James Tandy Brown. He married Alma Victoria Whelchel in 1909, and they had nine children, including Mora Esther Brown, my mother. My grandparents, Daddy Brown and Mama Brown, raised their family on a large farm in Knight's Bluff community, adjacent to Antioch community. The former Brown family farm is now part of Wright Patman Lake.

I walked over the Hill family farm as a young lad while hunting squirrels, and I went through the old residence. I remember the day that old house burned down; we saw the dense smoke from our house about a mile away. I visited Daddy Brown and Mama Brown at their farm on numerous occasions before the state bought all the farms in their area to make way for the huge lake. The Brown farm was located in the rich Sulphur River bottom land, and the old home site sits at the edge of the lake. Grandpa Hill died six years before I was born, so I never knew him, but I spent many happy times with Grandma Hill, Daddy Brown, and Mama Brown. I had wonderful grandparents.

I was born and spent the first few years of my life in a house located in Antioch community on a farm owned by one of Daddy's brothers, Uncle Charlie. Literally, I was born in that house rather than in a hospital; the doctor came to our house to help Mother give birth. That was the custom back then. Daddy and Uncle Charlie farmed together for a period of time, and Grandma Hill lived with us. They constructed a small home for Grandma Hill adjacent to Uncle Charlie's house, and she moved into it. Shortly thereafter, we moved to a tenant farm adjoining Uncle Charlie's farm, and I resided there until I graduated from high school in 1947. Our tenant farm was in the Knight's Bluff school district, so a majority of my childhood and school memories relate to that farm.

Cass County was predominately a farming region in the twenties and thirties. Cotton and corn were the major crops, and farmers did all work manually with the aid of horses and mules. People did not own automobiles in the twenties, so they traveled narrow dirt roads by foot, horseback, buggy, or wagon. Folks in my area began buying cars in the thirties, but it was not until World War II was well under way that a majority of the people owned cars. Roads were improved and widened, but very few rural roadways were paved before the late forties. I rode a school bus ten miles on a narrow dirt road until I graduated from high school in 1947.

I have little knowledge of the rural schools in Antioch, Knight's Bluff, Blalock, and Courtland communities during the twenties, but education was not a high priority for farmers back then. Almost everyone in my neck of the woods farmed, and education was of little benefit to people who plowed, chopped cotton, pulled corn, and picked cotton for a living. For them, it was more important for children to stay home and help with the farm chores than go to school. My father and mother obtained eighth grade and fifth grade educations, respectively, and they were among the lucky ones. A lot of parents did not send their kids to school at all.

My generation was the first to graduate from high school in significant numbers. We were the first to have school bus transportation to high schools in Queen City and Atlanta, so we were the first rural kids given a real opportunity to attend high school. My parents and their peers lived great distances from high schools, and they did not have cars or school bus transportation, so they could not have attended high school if they wanted to. The Great Depression of the thirties ended with the start of World War II. A lot of rural folks then worked in defense jobs, more people owned automobiles, and rural kids had access to school bus transportation, so kids on the farm attended high school in much greater numbers in the forties. A majority of my peers obtained a high school education, but most did not pursue a college degree.

None of the rural communities in our area had electricity in the twenties, so no one had running water and indoor bathrooms. Farmers obtained light from kerosene lamps, water from manual deep wells, heat from wood-burning heaters or fireplaces, and bathroom facilities from outhouses. The federal government began installing Rural Electric Administration (REA) power lines in rural areas in the thirties, but it was late in the forties before a majority of country folks had electric service. My family did not receive REA electric service until about 1950.

After receiving REA electric service, a lot of rural people installed electric pumps in their water wells, wired their houses, and built indoor bathrooms. Use of butane gas for cooking and heating also gained popularity in rural areas at about the same time. Employment in defense related jobs remained high, the overall economy was strong, VA home loans came into prominence, and people had money, so rural folks constructed modern homes in large numbers during the decade following World War II. So finally in the fifties, country folks were able to enjoy the modern conveniences of urban dwellers. It was in the early fifties that my parents bought their own farm, received their first home electric service, installed an electric pump in their well, added an indoor bathroom, and installed butane heaters and cook stove.

The rural economy in the twenties and thirties revolved around farming. Everyone lived on a farm, most had large families, and a majority of the children worked with their parents on the family farm until they married and started their own families. A few men did branch out into other lines of work, however. Local sawmills hired workers, some fulltime and others part-time. A few men sawed logs and hauled the logs to those local sawmills. Loggers sawed logs with a two-man crosscut saw and an axe, and "mule skinners" drug the logs to a truck using a mule or horse. The mule skinner placed a pole ramp on one side of the truck bed and drug the logs onto the truck, and the driver hauled the truck load of logs to a nearby sawmill.

A relatively small number of men specialized in building houses, or carpentry work, but that was most often a part-time profession. The demand for construction work was insufficient during that time period to provide fulltime work for carpenters. Three of my Brown uncles were excellent carpenters, but they also farmed to supplement their construction income. The pulpwood industry was new in our area, and a few men cut pulpwood for a living. Daddy and I cut pulpwood for a few weeks one winter to supplement our farm income, and I cut pulpwood one summer to earn extra money.

As more people bought cars, and as cars became more complicated, some men worked as automobile mechanics, but again, that mechanic work was primarily part-time. "Shade-tree" mechanics normally worked on people's cars under trees in the back yards of their farms; mechanic work was a spare-time activity for them. Most folks on farms kept milk cows, so they occasionally sold calves or cows. One or two men in our area bought and sold livestock for a living. They purchased the animals from farmers and took them to the weekly Douglasville livestock auction. I remember times when Mr. Holland, one of our neighbors, came to our house to pick up a young calf for the auction.

Religious activities were not a big part of our lives when I was growing up. Most communities had only one or two churches, and some had none, and people were scattered across a wide area without cars. Farmers were busy with their crops and other farm duties, so they had little time to spend in church. Sunday was also the only day in which folks could visit family, and most country churches could afford a preacher only two Sundays each month. Church was not a priority for most farm households, but they were God-fearing religious people. Rural folks believed in God and tried to live their lives in obedience to the teaching of the Bible. My parents were typical of their peers in matters of religion. Rather than talk a great deal about their religion, they lived it out in their lives. Their actions and attitude toward people reflected their faith.

Some of my neighbors lived in large houses, whereas others resided in small shacks. Most raised large families on sizeable acreage, but a few had small families on much smaller pieces of land. Our circumstances differed, and we were a diverse people, but we occupied the same station in life. We were poor and no one realized it. Rural farm life was the only life we knew, and none of us had been exposed to a higher standard of living. We were happy and content with our meager existence on the farm. It was only after we assimilated into an urban setting in the forties that farm folks recognized our substandard lifestyle and desired something better.

Rural farm life in the twenties and most of the thirties was a myriad of small worlds. Families were tied down to fulltime toil on farms, lack of transportation limited mobility, and a primitive news media limited interface with the outside world. Farmers in those days were essentially self-sufficient, requiring few goods and services from outside their communities. We raised a vast majority of our food, maintained our homes and farm equipment, doctored most of our ailments and illnesses, made most of the goods we consumed, and relied on extended family for needed help. We purchased a few staple groceries, limited clothing and household goods, necessary fertilizers and insecticides, occasional replacement farm implements, and not much else. Farm folks were an independent lot. That changed, though, as rural inhabitants began to take on defense related work outside their communities. We became more dependent on society as a whole.

Farm people in my youth thus dwelt in their own little world, interacted primarily with citizens from that world, and had minimal contact with those outside their domain. We were prejudiced against anyone different. My parents and their peers grew up in the backdrop of slavery, the Civil War, the very bitter Reconstruction era of the late 1800s, and the KKK, so they were especially biased against African Americans. That prejudice extended, however, to Hispanics, Jews, Catholics, and others. The South remained segregated after Reconstruction ended in 1877, so black people were forced to attend separate schools, use "Colored Only" water fountains and restrooms, ride in the back of buses, and wait in separate waiting rooms for trains and buses. Virtually all restaurants, movie theaters, ballparks, and other public facilities remained segregated throughout the thirties and forties.

In addition to segregation, white folks subjected African American citizens to all kinds of indignities and oppression. Slavery was long gone in our country, but Caucasians treated black people as if they were property with no human value. Only a few people physically abused African Americans or took advantage of them economically, and most white people I knew dealt with black folks with fairness and kindness. But, a majority of Caucasians looked on African Americans as an inferior race, not quite as good as white people. That attitude of superiority came through loud and clear to the black community, and one can imagine the hurt and indignities they suffered. Racial prejudice is one aspect of my upbringing for which I am ashamed.

Airplanes were uncommon sights for farm people in the thirties and early forties. About the only airplanes I remember seeing on the farm were small aircraft flown by federal agents searching for illegal whiskey stills in the wooded areas around our farm. Commercial aircraft carrying both people and cargo had been around throughout that time period, but the industry did not take off until the conclusion of World War II. Technology and hardware developed during the war, especially the B-29 bomber, were converted to commercial airline use, and large numbers of wartime pilots were eager to fly commercial airplanes. It was in the fifties that the commercial airline industry really took off. Of historical interest, Bessie Coleman received a lot of recognition as America's first African American pilot. She was born in Atlanta in 1892 and was a pioneer in the fledgling aircraft industry until her death in an airplane crash in 1926.

My parents' generation toiled on family farms prior to the Great Depression to eke out a meager living. They struggled for survival during the depression years of the thirties, demonstrating superior work ethics, resilience, perseverance, resourcefulness, integrity, and a strong will to survive. That generation could show people today a thing or two about money management and finances. They lived by an extremely simple but effective economic principle, "Do not spend more than you earn; make do with what you have." Folks back then paid cash for everything. They did not have home loans, automobile loans, revolving charge accounts, or credit cards. The only debt they incurred was for money to produce a crop the following year, and that debt was minimal. Their philosophy was, "If I do not have the money for a thing, I do not need that thing."

That Greatest Generation took on the challenge, the sacrifices, and the military human toll of World War II with honor and patriotism. Throughout their struggles, my parents and others like them strived to leave our country and our world in better condition than they found them. They labored and did without so their children, me and you, could enjoy a better life than they had. Theirs is a legacy I profoundly respect and cherish, and I pray I can leave the same kind of legacy for my daughter and grandchildren.

14.

A Look Forward

I have described various aspects of life on the farm in the twenties, thirties, and forties. Lean times of the twenties preceded terrible Great Depression years of the thirties, and the bloody World War II era brought an end to the devastating economic depression. My parent's generation, the Greatest Generation, helped our nation through those difficult times and left us with a country and a legacy we honor and cherish. Theirs was a manual existence lived out before development of the mechanized, automated, fast-track, high-tech society of today. My generation is a product of that somewhat primitive upbringing, but many of us have lived to see a transition to our present global economy and high-tech world.

What kind of legacy is my generation leaving, and what kind of society have we created together with our children and grandchildren? Have we retained the principles of living and character attributes of the Greatest Generation, or have we forgotten what they taught us and chosen different paths at times? Sadly, the lifestyles and priorities of people today are in stark contrast to those of my parent's generation. Our nation has evolved from a resourceful people of sacrifice to a me-first, I-want-it-now citizenry in seventy short years. Allow me to define that transformation as best I can and identify underlying factors contributing to the changes in attitudes and actions of our people.

A combination of happenings and developments brought us to where we are today. I will leave it to the sociologists to explain how the many complex events and technological advances of the last seven decades interacted to produce today's society. Suffice to say, the attributes, priorities, and actions of our people changed as our nation evolved. Rather than consider how society as a whole was transformed over the last seventy years, allow me to focus on different aspects of that evolution. For example, how did folks' view, or appreciation, of education change between 1940 and 2010?

A word of caution is in order at this time. All of our citizens were not alike during the Great Depression, and neither is everyone the same today. We can define the typical individual in the thirties and the average person today, but we must realize a lot of folks were not typical then and many are not average now. I will simply characterize various facets of our society as our nation evolved, realizing there are exceptions to that general characterization. In that way, I can draw a contrast between the attitudes, priorities, actions, and overall character of people in the thirties and folks today.

Every young man expected to serve time in the military when I was growing up; two or more years of military service was just a part of life. The men of our country willingly enlisted in our armed forces after Japan bombed Pearl Harbor. Most men felt a personal obligation to defend their country, to do their part; you could call that universal patriotism. World War II soldiers came from all walks of life and all economic levels of our society. Poor folks, rich people, farmers, bankers, factory workers, school teachers, movie stars, lawyers, salespeople, sports stars, and people of every ilk served side-by-side and shared foxholes. Military deferments were rare in the forties.

That willingness to serve in our military diminished markedly in subsequent wars. Quite a few young men obtained deferments during the Korean conflict, but it was in the Viet Nam War that large numbers of men found ways to avoid military service. Men from wealthy or politically connected families received multiple deferments or were assigned to stateside National Guard units. For the first time in our nation's history, masses of our young men shirked their responsibility to protect our country. Our wealthy citizens passed that responsibility to young men of moderate means. A significant number of Viet Nam era "draft dodgers" became presidents, vice-presidents, congressmen, governors, judges, and other leaders of our country. They wrap themselves in the flag, wear flag lapel pins, place

Support Our Troops decals on their cars, and masquerade as patriots.

The military discontinued involuntary conscription (the draft) after the Viet Nam War; America now has an all-volunteer armed forces. As a result, an overwhelming number of military recruits come from minority and low income segments of our population. Affluent families do not send their young men and women to war, but too many of them are gung-ho to send sons and daughters of less-affluent parents to do their fighting. That was true for the Gulf War in the early nineties, but is even more pronounced in current wars in Iraq and Afghanistan. That lack of personal responsibility in the area of military service permeates every facet of life. Discontinuing the draft did not build character in men and women of our country, but I firmly believe two or more years military service does build character.

All segments of our population supplied troops in World War II, and all classes of our citizens supported the soldiers with their resources. Wealthy people did not demand tax cuts and tax breaks; they willingly paid their fair share. Interest rates for war bonds were below the market rate, but ordinary folks scrimped and saved to buy savings stamps and war bonds. Singer Kate Smith and other Hollywood and sports stars raised huge sums of money for war bonds through marathon radio broadcasts and personal tours. Our government pleaded for its citizens to support the war effort financially, and the people responded by purchasing war bonds in large quantities. Men and a few women went off to war, masses of women joined the workforce, everyone conserved critical commodities, parents bought war bonds, kids collected scrap metal, and businesses produced war materials and equipment. In essence, all Americans sacrificed and did their part in World War II. Folks were truly patriotic.

What can we say about our country and the Iraq and Afghanistan wars of today? Americans' attitude toward, and prosecution of, our current wars is a sad commentary on our contemporary society. But let me say up front that our soldiers' performance in Iraq and Afghanistan has been outstanding, and their patriotism is without question. One can quarrel with the decisions made by our government and find fault with some of our military strategies, but no one questions our soldiers' dedication to duty and their performance.

That said, our government leaders refused to acknowledge the magnitude of the tasks and the costs of the wars in Iraq and Afghanistan. Rather than ask citizens to pay for the wars through higher taxes or by buying war bonds, our government borrowed hundreds of billions of dollars from foreign governments. Citizens other than our troops and their families have not shouldered the economic burden of war. It has been business as usual for the Wall Street crowd, the banking industry, the manufacturing segment, the service sector, the energy industry, the multitude of other businesses, and John Q. Public. People and corporations have made billions of dollars off the wars but have contributed nothing toward paying for the war efforts.

And, what about the tens of millions of self-proclaimed young patriots; why are they not stampeding to military recruiting offices? Congress does not have the will to consider restart of involuntary conscription, and a vast majority of our young men and women feel no obligation to serve in our military and defend our country. So, it falls on our volunteer soldiers to put their lives on the line, and it is their families who face the anguish of getting that dreaded visit from a military officer informing them of the death of their loved one. Ordinary citizens are not required or asked to support our nation's war effort with their money or service, and few do so voluntarily. I see little true patriotism in our citizenry. That is a far cry from our society of the forties.

Education was not high on the priority list for most rural folks in the thirties and early forties, especially for farmers and their families. Ours was essentially a manual economy, and minimal education was required to qualify for farm work, factory jobs, construction work, warehouse jobs, and a multitude of skilled and unskilled manual jobs. Technological advances after World War II, together with the G.I. Bill, prompted a lot of veterans and young people to pursue high school and college educations. A more mobile society and bountiful employment opportunities influenced an increasing number of rural young people to leave their family farms for more lucrative careers.

We have witnessed an almost unbelievable technological explosion over the last six decades. Black and white television entered into most homes in America, followed by stereo music systems, colored television, and now sophisticated entertainment centers. Manual math computations were replaced by slide rules, then scientific calculators, and finally complex computer systems. Vacuum tubes and discrete components gave way to semiconductors, followed by integrated circuits, and then complex integrated systems. Simple landline telephones were replaced by complex telephone systems, wireless telephone systems, cellular phones, and the computer based internet.

Compare the Ford Model T automobile I drove as a youngster to the computerized high-performance luxury cars of today, and contrast the propeller driven B-29 workhorse of World War II to sophisticated supersonic jet aircraft and spacecraft of today. Small banks of the thirties utilized manual bookkeeping systems, but they evolved into global computerized financial giants. Those and a host of other high-tech advances are products of an educated workforce, but the resulting space age world demands increasingly higher education levels to sustain growth. Education and technology thus produced a snowballing economy over the last six decades. Higher education levels led to greater technology development, which in turn, demanded higher educated workers.

The manual banking system of the thirties was quite simple and usually local. When a farmer or business needed money, they went to their local banker and obtained a loan, most likely a signature, or "hand-shake," loan. The farmer or business repaid the banker at the agreed time. Banks making the loans held home mortgages and automobile loans rather than selling them to third parties. Today's computerized global banking and finance industry is much more complex. Loans by banks and other financial institutions are "bundled" and traded like commodities. I am not sure anyone really understands our global banking and finance conglomerates, so today's financial system is rife with fraud and corruption. The global financial meltdown of the last two years is a stark reminder of our unstable financial world.

People's attitudes toward personal debt today are quite different from the attitudes of my parent's generation. Folks in the twenties and thirties hated debt, and they borrowed money as a last resort, usually from family members. A large number of farmers borrowed money each spring to plant and harvest crops, but that was the extent of their borrowing. They did without anything they were unable to pay for; people lived within their means. Home mortgages, automobile loans, and retail charge accounts were rare, and credit cards represented the future.

My generation's views regarding personal debt deviated from the views of our parents, but we held on to a lot of their economic principles. We took out home mortgages, but we purchased homes we could comfortably pay for with our levels of income. Most of my peers paid cash for their cars and home furnishings, although a few took out automobile loans and opened retail charge accounts. But again, most folks kept those time payments at comfortable levels and of short durations. People in the thirties were not obsessed with trying to keep up with or outdo their circle of friends or coworkers. They also sent their children to colleges they could afford; they did not take out student loans to pay for their children's education.

My wife and I saved until we could pay cash for a new car, requiring that we drive each car purchased eight to ten years. We purchased a number of automobiles over the years, and it was in 1989 that we purchased our first vehicle on time payment. The manufacturer offered two percent financing at the time, and it was less expensive to pay finance charges than pull money out of savings and lose interest income. We also saved and paid cash for our daughter's college education, negating the need for a burdensome student loan. My generation gradually began using credit cards, but we paid off the balances each month to prevent high interest charges and to ensure we were not overextended. My peers incurred moderate debt, but they did so judiciously.

What about our children, the so-called Baby Boomers, and our grandchildren? What is their view toward personal debt? They belong to what I refer to as the me-first, I-want-it-now generation, which seems to have no qualms about taking on huge debt to pay for extravagant lifestyles. Many of them buy larger than needed homes in prestigious neighborhoods, attend exclusive universities, own expensive automobiles and boats, buy all the latest high-tech gadgets, belong to prestigious country clubs, wear fashion clothes, dine at the finest restaurants, travel extensively, and maintain a fast-paced social life. And, they do so on credit. As a result, too many of our children and grandchildren are saddled with tens of thousands of student loan debts, huge home mortgage payments, sizeable home equity loans to pay off, large automobile and furniture payments, and tens of thousands of credit card balances.

Let me reiterate a key point. All members of a particular generation are not the same. A minority of folks in my generation did not carry on the tradition of our parents. Instead, they took on excessive debt to pay for things beyond their economic abilities. In a like manner, a lot of my generation's children and grandchildren lead financially responsible lives. They practice patience and self-control and do not spend money they do not have. We find a few folks in every generation who have the financial wherewithal to live extravagant lifestyles. Those lucky individuals live in whatever manner they choose without being burdened with excessive debt. My concern, however, is for the folks who have limited economic means but insatiable appetites for the finer things of life.

Today's society is plagued with a lack of personal financial responsibility, and our citizens also exhibit a deficiency in national financial responsibility. People want more from government than they are willing to pay for with taxes. Americans today insist on greater military spending, increased Social Security and Medicare benefits, an enhanced national infrastructure, higher welfare benefits, increased education spending, and more money for a host of other government funded programs. Yet, people demand cuts in taxes. And what do our politicians do? They give our citizens what they ask for, so our nation runs up budget deficits measured in trillions of dollars.

What are the underlying causes of such pronounced changes in our country over the last seventy years? Once again, I will leave it to the sociologists to answer that question, but allow me to offer a few suggestions. Families are no longer concentrated in close proximity, so they cannot depend on one another for support; folks turn to our government to meet their needs. My parent's generation worked hard in the thirties to survive, so they had good work ethics. Technology advances and a growing economy negated the need for a lot of people to perform hard manual labor to make a living, so work ethics gradually deteriorated over time. More and more of our citizens live off government handouts rather than the fruits of their labor, so the incentive to work is lower.

As America worked its way out of the Great Depression and recovered from World War II, profound changes began to take place in our society. Higher paying jobs and technological developments made life easier for our citizens, and they gained access to modern conveniences. Self-sacrifice of our people was replaced by selfishness, and character attributes of patience and perseverance gave way to instant gratification. And finally, honesty and integrity of our folks were supplanted by greed and corruption. That character degradation is apparent in the attitudes and actions of our people, and it is obvious in the conduct of our local, state, and federal government officials. The overall character of America has declined in the last seventy years.

15.

The End of the Story

You have accompanied me on my journey into the past. I have shared with you my early life on the farm and described what life on a Northeast Texas farm was like in the twenties, thirties, and forties. My upbringing and early life experiences were very much like those of hundreds of thousands of my peers on farms throughout the South. We lived in different places, belonged to different families, were a part of diverse cultures, raised a variety of crops, and had unique life experiences, but we shared a common lifestyle. All were poor, all worked hard, all learned to make do with what we had, and each was an offspring of the Greatest Generation. How did we turn out, how did we live as adults?

Allow me to review briefly what transpired in my life after I left the farm. I believe my story is representative of the life experiences of my generation of rural kids born in the thirties. I graduated from high school in 1947, as did a majority of my peers in that time period. Quite a few kids in my generation dropped out of school to help on their family farms or to seek employment elsewhere, but ours was the first generation to graduate from high school in large numbers. Fortunately, most of our parents recognized the benefit of a high school education and encouraged their children to stay in school.

I graduated from high school with no definite plans for my future. I did not consider going to college, and I had no dreams or aspirations regarding a possible career. I was happy and content living on a farm, and I enjoyed performing farm work, but I had a yearning for something different, a job away from the farm. I finished high school at fourteen years of age and moved to Atlanta to live with an aunt when I turned fifteen. I was unable to work in a factory environment because of contemporary child labor laws, so I took a job with Walker Drug Store as a soda jerk. I earned fifteen dollars per week for six ten-hour days, and I was flying high. I had money to spend and I could do as I pleased.

I went to work in a glove factory in Atlanta when I turned sixteen, the allowable age for factory work. I do not recall exactly what the pay was, but it was approximately fifty cents per hour for a forty-hour week. I was really rolling in dough then. I purchased a 1939 Ford sedan, started to drive, and moved back to the farm with my parents. That vehicle was a powerful machine with a sixty-five horsepower engine; I had to speed up approaching steep inclines in order to make it up the hills. I was just creeping along by the time I got to the top of the hills.

Soon after I got my wheels and before I drove very much, I went to Atlanta to apply for a driver's license. I passed the written test with flying colors, but then came the driving test and my downfall. The officer had me drive to a side street and told me to parallel park, and I really messed that up. He recognized that I was a novice driver at best and instructed me to drive back to his office. The officer gave me a beginner's permit, told me to drive straight home, and instructed me to come back after I learned to drive.

I never went back because I moved to Shreveport, Louisiana, shortly thereafter with Doyle, one of my cousins. Both of us went to work for the A&P Grocery Store chain, earning around a dollar an hour. Doyle worked in the grocery section initially, and I started out in the produce section. I transferred to a different store and moved to the grocery section after a few months. I was really in big money then. Doyle and I stayed with his older brother, Charles, and his family for a few months, rented a bedroom from a lady for a time, and moved into Mrs. Simmons' boarding house. Actually, she owned three houses, but meals were prepared and served in the main house.

Mrs. Simmons charged twelve dollars per week for room and board, including maid service. We slept three men to a room, and four rooms shared a bathroom containing one bathtub, one toilet, and a sink. You can imagine how filthy the bathtub was after use by twelve men, some of whom worked in dirty construction jobs. Our "home" wasn't exactly a five-star hotel, but we did get very good home-cooked meals, including sack lunches for residents who worked a great distance from the boarding house. Mrs. Simmons was a very nice lady, and she watched out for her "boys." A sad thing happened while we were living there though. Her alcoholic son lived there with his wife, and he blew his brains out one afternoon while sitting in his car in their garage. I visited Mrs. Simmons once or twice while on furlough from the Air Force.

Louisiana required only a written test for a driver's license, so I was able to obtain my license without taking a driving test, to my relief. Soon after moving to the big city of Shreveport, and before I obtained my driver's license, I was driving downtown one afternoon with Doyle riding shotgun. I saw a policeman ahead of us and I just knew he was going to arrest me for driving without a license. I panicked and made Doyle switch places with me while stopped at a traffic light. The boy was out of the country, but the country was not out of the boy. I was sixteen years old in a big city, fresh off the farm and not dry behind the ears yet.

I lived in Mrs. Simmons' boarding house about two years, until I enlisted in the Air Force. A few older construction workers boarded there, but most of the residents were young country boys like Doyle and me. We had a ball during those two years; something was always going on. Three of the young men formed a country music band, and they played almost every night, sometimes on the front porch or the upstairs balcony. I remember neighbors gathering on the front sidewalk to listen to the music. A group of us entered a team in the YMCA basketball league, and we swam a lot, enjoyed roller skating, and played tennis. Some of the guys played low-stakes poker almost every night, and three or four high-rollers started high-stakes games occasionally, which I never joined.

The Louisiana Hayride was a feature attraction in Shreveport during the forties and fifties. The Hayride was initiated in April, 1948. It was held in the Shreveport Municipal Memorial Auditorium and was broadcast each Saturday night on KWKH Radio and several other stations. The Louisiana Hayride quickly became the second most popular country music venue behind the

Grand Ole Opry. Stars who graced the stage of the Louisiana Hayride included Hank Williams, Kitty Wells, Jimmie Davis, Faron Young, Webb Pierce, and many others. A group of guys from the boarding house attended a lot of the Hayride shows, and I was there the night Hank Williams introduced his first big hit, "Lovesick Blues."

Those construction workers were an interesting lot. Three of them worked hard five days each week, received their pay on Friday, and loaded up on booze on Friday evening. They lay on their bunks all day on Saturday and Sunday and consumed their liquor. They filled trash cans with empty booze bottles by Monday morning and were off to work again. That was a weekly ritual for them. Those old guys did not bother anyone; they just drank themselves into a stupor every weekend. I do not know if they had wives and families or not; they kept pretty much to themselves. Other construction workers boarding there were ordinary folks; they joined in with the younger men in poker games and country music.

It was during that time in Shreveport that I discovered girls. I had gone out with girls a few times in Atlanta, but never really got into the dating scene. In Shreveport, I had a job, money in my pocket, a car, and a lot of places to meet the opposite sex. Most girls my age were still in high school, and a majority of them had ten o'clock curfews. I often dropped a date off at curfew time and headed to a club in Bossier City for two or three hours of dancing. Two dates in one night was thus not unusual for me. The hick from the sticks was somewhat citified. At other times, I dropped dates off and joined poker games in progress at the boarding house and played until early morning hours.

I recall one curfew I missed. I was dating a girl in high school regularly, and her father imposed a strict ten o'clock curfew. I took her to a movie one night and it turned out to be an unusually long movie. I believe it was "Samson and Delilah," a classic. Anyway, I got my date home well past her curfew. Her father was known to tip the bottle pretty heavy, and he was drinking that night. Her mother told us he was out looking for his little girl. We explained why we were late, and her mother told me to leave and that she would take care of it with him. My date's father never mentioned the incident to me, so I suppose he was satisfied with our explanation.

A lot of country guys like me moved to Shreveport during the forties, and a large number of country gals moved there too. Girls on the farm were no longer satisfied with working on a farm with their families or marrying young and working on a farm with their husbands. Rural girls graduated from high school, and many of them moved to the city to find careers. As a result, Shreveport contained an ample supply of young telephone operators, business school students, nursing school trainees, and other single ladies preparing for careers. Those female hicks from the sticks were rapidly becoming acclimated to life in the city. Pickings were thus good for a young man with a job, a car, and money to spend.

You have heard it said that there is no honor among thieves. Well, there was no honor among that boarding house gang either. If one of the guys was dating a girl and left for a week or two on vacation, guess what! Another guy would fill in for him and date his girl while he was gone. I have been known to do such a dastardly deed. Boarding house life definitely was not boring, and I have fond memories of the great guys I met during those two years. We visited back and forth with each other's families on the farm during weekends. I recently visited the boarding house I called home sixty years ago. It has since been remodeled and converted into a family residence.

Doyle and I and two of our buddies volunteered for the Air Force before we were to be drafted into the Army. That was during the Korean conflict. I received basic training at Lackland Air Force Base in San Antonio before being shipped to Keesler Air Force Base in Biloxi, Mississippi, for radar maintenance school. I met Dot Cothran while stationed at Keesler AFB, and we married just before I was transferred to Barksdale Air Force Base in Bossier City. I spent two hitches at Barksdale AFB and another hitch back at Keesler AFB for advanced radar maintenance school before I was assigned to Lauighlin Air Force Base in Del Rio, Texas. Our daughter, Debbie, was born while I was stationed at Barksdale AFB. I was discharged from the Air Force at Laughlin AFB in July, 1955, we moved to Baton Rouge,

Louisiana, and I enrolled in Louisiana State University (LSU) in September.

I enjoyed my four-year tour in the Air Force, but it was very much like a job. I lived off base after I married and commuted to work each day. I even worked part-time at the A&P Grocery Store where I was employed before enlisting in the Air Force. It was in the Air Force that I was initiated into electronics. I never planned to go to college, but my acquired interest in electronics and the G.I. Bill led me to choose electronics engineering as a career. I was eight years removed from high school when I enrolled at LSU, but my four years of electronics training and maintenance experience aided me greatly in my studies at LSU. A lot of my classmates were fellow veterans and former farm boys, so we developed close friendships while at LSU.

My academic experience in a one-room, one-teacher elementary school and a small high school was in no way detrimental to my earning an engineering degree. I finished at the top of my electronics engineering class and received a number of job offers. I chose Collins Radio Company outside of Dallas, Texas. I was subsequently employed by three electronics companies in Dallas and Houston over the next seventeen years, including the last ten years with Texas Instruments. I left Texas Instruments to open a retail bicycle shop, Bicycle World, in Houston. I loved engineering work, but I had a yen to run my own business, and bicycles presented a promising future in 1974.

I ran Bicycle World for twenty-two years, during which time our daughter, Debbie, married Glenn Johnson, moved to Austin, Texas, and gave birth to our granddaughter, Jennifer, and our grandson, David. My wife and I retired in 1996, sold Bicycle World and our Houston home, and moved to Taylor, Texas, outside of Austin. We chose Taylor because it is in the midst of a farming region similar to Northeast Texas where I grew up. We enjoy seeing the farmers plant, cultivate, and harvest their cotton and corn crops each year. Farming is done on a much larger scale today, and none of the work is done manually anymore, but the cotton and corn fields are just as pretty as they were seventy years ago.

Our retirement years are typical for my generation. We stay busy with church activities, charity work, senior adult social activities, gardening, and visiting children and grandchildren. I have also written and published four books since I retired. My wife, Dot, succumbed to lung cancer in early 2004 after almost fifty-two years of marriage. I met a wonderful widow lady a few months later, and Aileen Maynard and I married in late 2005. Jennifer, my granddaughter, gave birth to a boy, Parker, in January, 2010, so I am a great-grandfather.

My wife, Aileen, grew up on a cotton and corn farm near Holland, Texas, about fifty miles Northeast of Austin. Her experience on the farm is virtually identical to mine. She knows all about a house with no electricity, making do with what you have, chopping cotton, pulling corn, picking cotton, tending to chickens and livestock, washing clothes on a rub board, gardening, canning vegetables and fruits, Sears & Roebuck catalogs in outhouses, warming by a fireplace, drawing water from a well, and all the other non-conveniences of rural life in the thirties and forties. A hick from the Northeast Texas sticks is very compatible with a hick from the Central Texas sticks.

My adult life has been influenced a great deal by the example set by my parents. I am grateful they taught me the value of honesty, integrity, hard work, resourcefulness, perseverance, compassion, generosity, and love of family. My lifestyle changed considerably as technology advanced and society kept pace, but I held on to my parents views about material possessions and debt. The same can be said for a majority of my peers who were raised on a farm in the thirties and forties.

I paid my way through college, aided by the G.I. Bill, without incurring debt, but I worked part-time while in school. We bought our first home, an economical house well within our price range, using a low-interest VA loan, and we paid off the thirty-year mortgage in seven years. Our second home in Houston was a lot larger, but well within our economic means, and we paid off the mortgage on it in eleven years. Upon retirement, we sold our home in Houston and paid cash for a somewhat smaller home in Taylor. My peers do not like debt, so most of them also owned homes with no mortgage balances by the time they were sixty years of age or younger. Not so, however, for our children, the Baby Boomers. Large numbers of them carry sizeable home mortgage balances, as well as home equity loan balances, into retirement.

My generation purchases flat screen televisions, computer systems, digital cameras, iPods, and other high-tech conveniences, but we do not demand the latest Gee Whiz gadgets, and we pay cash for them. We also carry credit cards in our wallets and use them for a large portion of our purchases. But, most of us pay off our credit card balances each month, unlike our children and grandchildren who often carry credit card balances measured in tens of thousands of dollars and higher. Like our parents, my generation has the patience and self-control to hold off on purchase of a "thing" until we can afford it, and if we cannot afford that thing, we do not really need it.

You are probably wondering about my spiritual life as an adult. My involvement in religion after graduating from high school and leaving the farm probably mirrored that of thousands of other rural high school graduates who moved to the city. I attended church occasionally from the time I moved away from home until I enlisted in the Air Force, but I was completely away from church during my first few months in the service. I then met the girl I was to marry while stationed at Keesler AFB, and I attended church regularly with her after we started dating. Dot was the daughter of a deacon, and regular church attendance was mandatory for her.

Dot and I married prior to my transfer to Barksdale AFB, and we gradually drifted away from church for the duration of my military service. Dot attended church occasionally with our daughter, but I seldom accompanied them. During my three and one-half years at LSU, Dot and our daughter, Debbie, were very active in a small church near the campus, and I got involved as well. We developed close friendships in Calvary Baptist Church. We moved to Richardson, Texas, outside of Dallas, in 1959 after I graduated from LSU.

Our church involvement was irregular during the next twenty-two years. Dot and Debbie attended church quite a lot during that time period, but I seldom joined them. Dot and I had drifted almost completely away from church by the time I was forty-nine years old. Then, she was diagnosed with extremely serious cancer. The doctors gave her a thirty percent chance of survival, and they started her on a one-year radiation and chemotherapy treatment routine. That changed our life outlook drastically.

I promised Dot I would take her to church and Sunday school. She joined a small Baptist church in Houston, and we attended Sunday school and worship service every Sunday. I studied my Bible daily for the next eleven months and accepted Jesus Christ as my Savior and Lord just before my fiftieth birthday. I have been heavily involved in church work the last twenty-seven years, teaching adult Bible study classes, serving as a deacon, and participating in various church ministries. God has richly blessed me, and I regret not serving Him in my younger adult years.

I have shared my story and my life experiences with you in this book, but I have also related to you the life experiences of hundreds of thousands of rural folks raised in the thirties on farms throughout the South. Our parents, the Greatest Generation, set an example for us, and they left us a legacy we honor and cherish. They struggled, sacrificed, and survived in the midst of extreme hardships and instilled in us character traits which serve us our entire lives. Our lives and accomplishments pale in comparison to those of our parent's generation, but we are better people because of the precedent set by them. Thank you, the Greatest Generation, and may we pass just a little of the character you exhibited on to our children and grandchildren.

CPSIA information can be obtained at www.ICGtesting.com
Printed in the USA
LVOW06s0551101013

356281LV00002B/6/P